Life Choices:
Navigating Difficult Paths

What Others Are Saying About This Book:

At a time in our country when bleakness is prevalent, how uplifting to have a book which shares positive turning points in people's lives. A most worthwhile read.

—Jack Sheehan, Author
Quiet Kingmaker of Las Vegas; The Class of '47; Skin City

In strange and uncertain times, such as those we now live in, you will find hope and encouragement in this wonderful book.

—Patricia Fripp, Past President, National Speakers Association
Author, *Get What You Want*

This book is about ordinary people succeeding in extraordinary ways, turning tragedy into triumph, seizing the opportunity before it ceases to be one, getting up one more time than you fall. It is filled with creative ideas, strategy and inspiration in the form of life stories that just may strengthen your own resolve to follow the path of 'Conquistador.'

—Doc Blakely, CSP, CPAE, Hall of Fame Professional Speaker
www.docblakely.com

Life Choices is a superb compilation of tales from people who overcame adversity and took control of their lives. The heartfelt stories prove once again what we can accomplish with prayer and a steadfast attitude to never give up.

—Peter Fogel, Speaker, Copywriter, Author
If Not Now... Then When? Stories and Strategies of People Over 40 Who Have Successfully Reinvented Themselves

The choices you made and the choices you didn't have brought you to this point. Since our lives truly are what our choices make them, we have a vital interest in making better choices. Let the compelling stories in this book expand your awareness and help you choose the right path for your life.

—Jim Cathcart, Founder, host of www.Motivation.tv,
Author of fifteen books, including: *The Acorn Principle*

These stories will fill a void of despair with the light of the lives that surround it. Stories of strength, courage and endless faith. Do not pass go; go directly to the cashier and buy it.

—Manuel Diotte, Motivational Teacher and Author
Happiness Is A Pair of Shorts

The choices we make along life's journey can either strengthen or weaken our inner foundations in which all character is built. This book gives first hand accounts of how we are all capable of making those choices that fortify our inner foundations, making way for a fortress of character. I recommend it to all who want to know how to transform "every" life experience into the building tools for such worthwhile construction projects.

—John Michael Stuart, MSW, Author, *Perfect Circles: Redefining Perfection*

This book draws from human experience that is alternately beautiful, miraculous and uplifting ~ and often all three at once. If you have ever asked yourself can I do this ~ and doubted that you could ~ you must read this book. The people here are real; their stories will answer your question with clarity and force: yes you can!

—Gail Cohen, Author, *Thinking Outside The Lines,
How To Reach Your Personal Best*

WOW! What an awesome reminder of the unseen, quintessential power living inside us! Thank you for sharing your life changing stories with us—it is warm, true and inspirational. It has given me the courage to embrace my "weakness" and my story ... for it has made me realize that actually it is my strength!! Life is a Gift! And we get to unwrap it every day—if we choose to ... Please choose to!!

—Marisa Wollheim, Director, Hospice in the West,
Krugersdorp, South Africa

After reading the stories in "Life Choices" I was uplifted and encouraged. We all have challenges and circumstances in life that are overwhelming. However, we all have the ability to overcome the seemingly impossible of circumstances. By reading these stories you'll be reminded of the inner strength we all possess and have the courage to evaluate your current situation and make a choice to follow the life you were meant to have.

—Peggy S. Vasquez
Certified Executive Administrative Professional (CEAP)
Executive Assistant to the Laboratory Director
Pacific Northwest National Laboratory

Life Choices

Navigating Difficult Paths

Anne Abernathy	Judi Moreo
Nancy Todd	Jennifer Joseph
Sandra Nielsen	Cattel
Victoria Lane	Sandy Kastel
Stephen Philpott	Anne Dreyer
Casey McNeal	Karen Phillips
Mary Monaghan	Sherial Bratcher
Susan Haller	Deborah Clark
Andrea Chestnut	Edie Raether
Jesse Ferrell	Dan Roberts
Jennifer Tarlin	Aimmee Kodachian
Elle Swan	Bob Walker
Ginette Osier Bedsaul	Charlotte Foust

LAS VEGAS, NEVADA

Copyright ©2010 by Turning Point International
All rights reserved.

No portion of this book may be reproduced in any form or by any means without permission in writing from the publisher, except for the inclusion of brief quotations in a review.

Editor: Jami Carpenter
Cover design and typesetting: Julia Lauer

Library of Congress Control Number: 2009940194
ISBN: 978-0-9825264-0-8

Post Office Box 231360
Las Vegas, Nevada 89105

www.lifechoicesbook.com

Published in the United States of America

Choices! We have choices. They are the source of the success in our lives. When things happen to us, we can choose to believe they happened for a reason. We can discover opportunities in the most difficult experiences if we are willing to look for them. It is what we choose to think about each experience that determines how we respond to it. How we respond determines whether or not we find richer, more purposeful, more joyful lives. We are the only ones who can choose our attitudes and the principles that we live by. Choose well, my friends. Choose well.

—From *Attitude is a Choice*

Contents

Introduction ix

Love
Jennifer Joseph – *Follow Your Heart* 12
Sandra Gore Nielsen – *A True Love Story* 21

Inspiration
Cattel – *The Mystical Hand of Freedom* 28
Vickie Lane – *Yes, It's Cancer* 34

Family
Sandy Kastel – *Detours* 46
Stephen Philpott – *Life of Success on My Own Terms* 58

Empower
Anne Dreyer – *Class is a Choice* 68
Casey McNeal – *The Circle of Influence* 77
Karen Phillips – *7 Keys 2 Success* 88

Courage
Susan Haller – *Life Forced* 100
Mary Monaghan – *New Beginnings* 107

Hope
Sherial Bratcher – *Creating My Dream Life* 114
Andrea Chestnut – *A Better Way to Live* 120

Opportunity
Deborah Clark – *There's a Story for That* 126
Edie Raether – *When Opportunity Knocks* 132
Judi Moreo – *The Choice That Changed My Life Forever* 139

Independence
Jesse Ferrell – *Defining Moment: You are Fired* 148
Dan Roberts – *George, Martha, and I* 156
Jennifer Tarlin – *A New Life* 163

Challenge
Nancy Todd – *Playing the Hand You're Dealt* 168
Aimmee Kodachian – *Finding My Purpose* 178

Experience
Anne Abernathy – *Why Not?* 186
Elle Swan – *The Best of You* 192
Bob Walker – *What Was I Thinking? Confessions of an Avid Adventurer* 198

Spirituality
Ginette Osier Bedsaul – *An Enacted Miracle* 204
Charlotte Foust – *Invisible* 213

A Final Thought 220

Introduction

We all have challenges in our lives. Sometimes we don't see them coming. Sometimes we invite them in. Some are bigger than others. Sometimes they come one right behind the other. Sometimes they show up all at once. Sometimes we have to make a choice in how we deal with these challenges.

This empowering collection of stories reminds us that we all have choices, and the choices we make are what determine the course of our lives. The authors of these stories are real people who have reached into the depths of their souls to share their inspiring journeys when navigating the difficult paths of their lives. These extraordinary people have persevered against the odds and made choices that enabled them to achieve successful lives. Through their experiences, we can find many important lessons to help us avoid wrong turns and blind alleys. Their stories show us that we can overcome our challenges and live more satisfying, passion filled lives.

If you feel "stuck" in a situation that appears to be beyond your control, these stories will show you how others have coped with crisis and uncertainty, made tough choices and positive changes in order to find deeper meaning and satisfaction in their relationships and learned to live with purpose every day.

Rarely do we find a book that addresses so many different challenges. *Life Choices* does this in a powerful and inspiring way. This book is about experiences, the people who lived them, and how they created successful lives. From values and self-fulfillment to legacy, this book offers new resources for people who have tough choices to make every day.

Filled with wisdom and love, this book is a soothing companion for anyone searching for the courage to make a choice to change his or her circumstances. These authors and their stories prove beyond a shadow of a doubt that success belongs to everyone, no matter where they come from or what has happened to them. They are living proof that miracles can and do happen.

You can be one of these people. You can navigate through difficult times and find your pathway to the life you choose to lead. Put the strength of others to work for you. Courage is not the absence of fear or pain. Courage is taking the steps to move through it.

Judi Moreo
President
Turning Point International, Inc.

Love

It's not hard to make choices when you know what your values are.

—Roy Disney

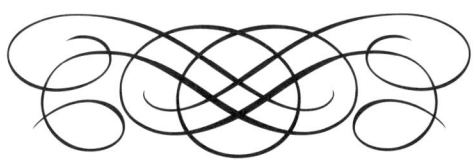

Follow Your Heart

JENNIFER JOSEPH

It was a beautiful day in New York City; I mean gorgeous. It was early fall and we got lucky with the weather. When I went outside for my morning coffee, the gentle breeze caressed my skin and the sun was shining brightly, ever so warm as it danced across my face. It was about eighty-five degrees, no humidity and not a cloud in the sky. I took my coffee and went back into my luxurious hotel room in a high-end area of Manhattan. My boyfriend (we'll call him Bob) was there on business and I tagged along, which I often did. It was a lot of fun. He was a good man who adored me. Bob was a bigwig in the music business, so we would fly first class, stay in beautiful hotels, hang around amazing rock and pop stars (some I grew up listening to and idolizing). I experienced all the behind-the-scene happenings of that world that average people typically never hear about. As a singer and performer myself, I was living what looked like a dream … why wasn't I happy?

A bit of background may shed some light on my feelings. A child of divorced parents, I lived with my mom, who at twenty-eight, was trying to figure out her own life. We didn't have much money, but she made it work. I remember that we ate a lot of Campbell's soup! My dad didn't pay child support or make regular appearances, though when he did show up, I was in absolute heaven. He was charming, good-looking, fun, and exciting. When he was there, it was like my prince charming came to find me. Even as a child I was a romantic. As an adult, I learned my dad was also irresponsible, unconventional, and a dreamer. Those weren't terrible things. What was terrible was that his lack of presence and the constant disappointments led me to believe for decades that I wasn't worthy.

Even when I was as young as seven, I compared myself to the other little girls. They were prettier, funnier, thinner, more gifted. I figured if I were like them, maybe I would be happy, because happy I was not. I was painfully shy and just didn't have a lot of friends. In my young mind I thought if I had both parents maybe that would make the difference. I constantly felt "less than." How does such a young child define depression? I didn't even know the word back then. I didn't have any foundation of strength so I held everything inside. My mom, in later years, said I was her fairy child and that she had always felt I could take care of myself. She didn't realize I desperately craved the attention which she wasn't capable of giving at that time. I knew she loved me, but she was stoic. That's how she was raised. Most times, I felt like a stranger in my own life. That definitely became my theme.

When I was nine, my mom remarried, which seemed to make her very happy. Even at six, when she had told me we were moving in with him, I knew it was a good stability move. I thought everything would be okay because we would be a family … and I would have a dad. Not so.

Seeing her happy made me feel good, but being with him didn't make me happy. This man was the polar opposite of my father. I thought that was ok—maybe one day he'd actually like me enough to really be my dad. Instead, I felt like I was a necessary evil, a bother, and not his daughter at all. I wanted ever-so-badly to feel that unconditional love of a father from him. It wasn't his fault; he was a good man and was taking wonderful care of my mom. I just needed so much more.

My stepdad was young and in a stressful job. He grew up believing children were meant to be seen, not heard; his lack of interest in me often reminded me of that. Needless to say as a young girl whose own father wasn't around much, I was always looking for my stepdad's love along with his attention and approval. He often teased me about my clumsiness, my answers to his questions, and remarked that I was lazy. I was so intimidated I would say foolish things, mess up even the simplest of tasks, and often stutter when I talked. He didn't know that he (along with my absentee father) was laying the foundation for my future insecurities and difficult relationships. My mom and stepdad eventually had a son, which made me even more of an outsider to the threesome they became. It's ironic; my brother once told me he didn't like me because I was the bad kid and he didn't want that association. He was the golden child. I felt so alone!

I struggled with this need for approval for the next twenty-five years. I spent my adolescence constantly lacking in self-esteem and filled my time with visions of a better life, set of parents, mind, voice, face, body—a better everything. At fifteen, I developed a bad case of bulimia, a prison I would fall in and out of for twelve years. I wouldn't wish that on anyone. Food filled the emptiness and eased the pain of feeling alone in the world, but then I would have to purge because I didn't know how to accept the nurturing I was trying to give myself. Food was definitely my closest friend and my worst enemy. You may not know, but that particular eating disorder doesn't make you thin. By the time I was seventeen, I ballooned to well over 200 pounds.

I was a decent student until I was in high school. Then I did what I absolutely had to in order to get by. I was uninterested in the subjects and quite frankly didn't care about the future. I would sneak out of my window at night and party with my friends who were older. Not coming in until late, I slept my way through the first few classes. My participation in choir was probably the only thing keeping me in school. Only by the grace of God, did I graduate.

No matter what I accomplished, I felt like a failure. I daydreamed a lot during school. I was scared. I became at expert at visualization, a skill that served me well later on in life.

Television was also a close friend of mine. It was a distraction from the negativity inside my head. I loved all the programs, especially the Miss America pageant. Year after year, while cheering for my favorite contestants, I would imagine what it would be like to be thin, pretty, and actually be on that stage. The one thing I loved to do more than anything was sing. I knew that if I were a contestant, singing would be my talent. Every night in my bedroom, I'd emulate Linda Ronstadt, Barbra Streisand, and Whitney Houston at the top of my lungs. While performing in my room, I visualized myself on the Miss America stage and other stages, as well, singing to crowds of thousands. Who would have guessed that this clumsy and awkward girl with no confidence to speak up would one day be on that very same stage and on many, many more?

At eighteen, I was living on my own, trying to figure out life, one mediocre job and one bad date at a time. Coincidentally, an acquaintance of mine, whom I respected and eventually became one of my very best friends, heard me rehearsing for a cruise ship talent show that I was going to perform in with another friend. She asked what I was doing with that talent. I said I didn't know; nothing that I knew of really. At that very moment, I was tipping the scales at 235 pounds. She said, "Honey, you're great! Lose that weight and you could sing for a living."

Wait ... WHAT?

ME? Actually on stage singing ... for a living? All I can say is that God works in mysterious ways. That vote of confidence was all I needed. Ten months later I had lost one hundred pounds.

I was determined to be healthy so I lost the weight the old fashioned way ... diet and exercise. I promised myself I was through with the binging and purging! I educated myself on nutrition, ate healthy, cut out sodas and juices, and drank only water, iced tea, and coffee. I never ate three to four hours before bed and I walked whenever I could. I was truly on a mission for me! I achieved the weight loss because I kept visualizing the outcome. I didn't focus on what I looked like each day because that would have sabotaged my success. I had my eye on the "future me." I knew I would achieve my goal.

Even after I reached my goal weight and my body had been transformed, my heart and mind were still the same. It became my life's quest to transform those as well. That's a hurdle many people are challenged with when trying to keep weight off for good.

I was almost twenty when all the excess pounds were off, yet in my eyes I was still 235 pounds, shy and insecure. No one would have ever guessed. I met a woman who said I could create my own reality in my mind and when I did that, it would happen in the world before me. She also told me to "Fake it 'til you make it," and "Be that on the outside which you strive to truly be inside and it will eventually happen authentically." I worked that theory and that is what started my true transformation.

At that time, I was stumbling my way through college, taking a course here and there, but I had no passion or drive for it. What I did have a passion for was singing so I frequented karaoke bars (sneaking in at nineteen) and found my other passion—performing live. I know it's weird for a shy girl to want to be a performer, but not really. Behind a microphone I could pretend to be someone else. It was a strange protective barrier for me but it worked. People actually started noticing me for my talent and I blossomed. I grew more confident. That started the new direction of my career and my life.

When I was almost twenty, I was hired to sing with a band that played the lounges in Las Vegas. I sang with them for three years, barely making money to pay my bills, loving every minute of it, still not finishing college. A girlfriend suggested that I compete for Miss Las Vegas, a preliminary for the Miss America scholarship pageant to help pay for college. I figured, "Why not?" I knew I would be uncomfortable walking in a bathing suit and heels in front of all those people, but I did it anyway. I wanted that scholarship. Guess what? I actually won! I went on to win the title of Miss Nevada as well and three months later, I was living my dream of singing on the Miss America stage in front of thousands. I even won the talent award! With the foundation of performing and the growth through the Miss America program, my life was beginning to take shape. My visualization was becoming my reality.

The years that followed had their ups and downs. Yes, so did my weight. It didn't help being in the entertainment field focused 24/7 on weight and image. I was often chastised and threatened with my job for being ten pounds overweight. I struggled with bouts of depression and bulimia again, which kept me from advancing in my career. My prison keeper was now my mind, not a parent who didn't know better.

I was horribly embarrassed about my dysfunction and did everything in my power to manage it. To everyone else, I looked as though I had it all together. I would often ask myself, "With everything I am starting to accomplish, why do I still despise myself and feel so horribly alone?" This self-hate led to more setbacks. I craved success and happiness so I kept persevering. I spent every bit of my twenties trying to heal my broken spirit through every self-help book, CD, and special herb I could find. I just wanted to feel "normal." Later in my life, a therapist I worked with and admired told me that "normal is just a setting on a washing machine." Oh, how right she was!

Finally, in my early thirties, through all my work on myself, my mindset was changing. All the work was paying off! It seemed like a constant one-step-forward, two-steps-back dance routine. Through much study and practice, I learned to love myself. I now know this is all a journey and not a race. I no longer need outside validation. I made bold changes and took risks in my career and stopped trying to fit into a mold. Then came a request from a producer I knew for me to perform a tribute to Linda Ronstadt. I traveled the country with the world famous *Legends in Concert* show for several years and loved every minute. Again, the world I had created in my mind so long ago had become a reality. I knew I had much to offer the world; I just needed to let go and let God take over. My life was becoming extraordinary.

Instead of achieving "normal," I was learning to love my quirks and differences, and my life was becoming better and better. I was learning to embrace the feeling of being a stranger in the world. I was learning to be an observer experiencing life rather than being attached to it. I was learning to love where I came from and live life to its fullest, to understand we're all one and on the same path to ultimate inner peace and happiness. I was learning forgiveness and understanding for myself and others. That released the chains of resentment and bitterness that were holding me and allowed me to have more love, compassion, and understanding of people. Even though I treasure my talent as a singer, I treasure these gifts of love, understanding, and compassion more. I have learned to appreciate what God brings me next, even the challenges and heartaches (and there have been many) for it's all a part of my growth! I honor those who have given me the obstacles in my life.

Now I practice gratitude every day. This practice has literally saved my life and every relationship I cherish. I'm very close with all three of my parents, and my brother loves and appreciates me now! When I no longer needed approval and validation, I got both. My parents have even stopped asking me when I am going to get a real job. They have truly shown me they are proud of what I have become! It all emanates from

Life Choices: Navigating Difficult Paths

the inside. It took a lot of work to transform the life of a young girl with no future to one of endless opportunities and success. I can live it all authentically now. We all have the choice to make those transformations.

Remember Bob and the New York hotel room? Well, there I was with all the financial security in the world, the availability of anything I could want, having an intimate love affair with the music business I craved, a very good man who loved me as well as he knew how, but I didn't have him. His work did. He was a self-proclaimed workaholic. After all the progress that I made on myself through personal development I was happy with who I had become. And yet, I was settling.

My voice in my head kept asking how selfish I was that I wanted it all. Here was this wonderful man offering me security. I would never have to worry about my next job or meal, but it would be on his terms. I didn't want his success. I wanted my own, so I made the decision to follow my heart and not "settle." I knew the break-up would be difficult, yet I had made a decision to close this chapter. Even with my decision, some self-doubt kicked in. That voice asked questions like, "What will my family say? What will his friends and family say? How can you leave when it's not "bad," but it's just not "good?" I chose not to listen to that voice. I found the strength and made the choice to move forward with my life.

As my mindset, self-confidence, and energy were changing from getting out my relationship with Bob, unbeknownst to me at the time, I met the man of my dreams. It was on a flight I wasn't even supposed to be on. At the last minute, I had decided to take a quick trip to Phoenix. I was exhausted and I shouldn't even have gone, but I did. On the return trip, I sat next to a total stranger who smiled and spoke to me. I was drawn to him like a magnet. As we talked, I found out he lived right around the corner from me! We became fast friends and started to see each other on a casual basis. As I got to know him, he lit a fire in me that hadn't been ignited in a long time. He was divorced and an exceptional father to his two children. He was positive, handsome, talented, intelligent, had a ton of integrity, and was so exciting. He was like Superman to me. He electrified my life by his mere presence and motivated me to no extent. These very intense feelings scared me so I kept a safe distance. Bob had been so safe and predictable. This man was a potential heartbreak waiting to happen, but I heard that voice deep down inside, "Make the choice. Take the risk," it said. I decided to listen this time.

He is everything I've ever dreamed of and more. We are deeply and passionately in love with immense respect and appreciation for each other. We've both learned so much from our past experiences and have extraordinary outlooks on life coupled with astounding communication which only deepens the connection. Where this will go, only God knows. I hope it lasts forever. If it doesn't, I know I'll be more than okay and God will bring the next big adventure. What I do know for sure is that our dreams are out there waiting for us. We just have to reach for them. Sometimes they're just around the corner!

My career seemed to follow suit. There have been changes and will be more. Life has never been better. I feel I have the world at my feet with more options than ever before because my mind is open to new possibilities.

It's interesting that when we decide to really live our lives the way we want, joy seeps into every single aspect of it. If I had to repeat all that I did to live life to its fullest, or my definition of it anyway, I'd be glad to. It was worth every moment. I feel like life is just beginning … again. I'm starting another brand new chapter in my journey.

In my life, the choice to follow my heart, even though it might have been the difficult road, always turned out to be the right direction. As I move through my life's journey, I live by four principles for success:
1. Follow your heart
2. Settling doesn't leads to happiness
3. Visualization leads to reality
4. Something better is just around the corner

One of my favorite quotes: Everything you ever desire is just outside your comfort zone!

About the Author

At nineteen, Jennifer Joseph arrived on the world famous stages of her hometown, Las Vegas, performing with a popular lounge band. After winning the title of Miss Nevada 1995 and receiving the talent award at Miss America, she went on to headline many shows around the world, including *Legends in Concert*, *Follies Bergere*, and her self-titled one-woman show. Jennifer received the rarely-given standing ovation on Showtime at the famous Apollo Theatre in Harlem, New York. She has also worked with Wayne Newton and opened for the legendary Don Rickles for almost two years. Until July 2010, you can find her starring in the high energy "Show in the Sky" at the Rio Hotel and Casino in Las Vegas, where Jennifer still calls home. Miss Joseph is very involved in many philanthropic organizations in the community as well as in helping young women achieve their personal goals in the Miss America pageant system(s).

Jennifer Joseph can be contacted at:
Turning Point International
P. O. Box 231360
Las Vegas, Nevada 89105
(702) 896-2228

A True Love Story

SANDRA GORE NIELSEN

"All you need is love…"
—Lennon and McCartney, Magical Mystery Tour

Any psychic will tell you what's on women's minds: "When will I find true love? Will I ever meet my soul mate? When will I not be alone?"

Love, money and health are the three pillars of a perfect life. But our true nirvana is a magical and elusive state of mind we call "Happiness." Of the three pillars, there is only one that alone can bring you even close to being happy.

Money can't buy love, but it can get you invited to some really good parties. It even goes a long way to buying health if you take advantage of organic foods, vitamin infusions, Mayo Clinic doctors, and personal trainers. Money we never take for granted, never have enough, and work hard at keeping.

Health we take for granted and should work hard at keeping. Life is a struggle with poor health. But even with our well-functioning bodies, how much fun is it to be healthy alone? Or rich alone? Or powerful alone? Anything alone?

Love makes all else worthwhile. It is the warmth that begins deep in our beings and emanates wide, for all the world to see that we are, indeed, happy.

What I have always known to be true is that love is what I need. Call me a hopeless romantic, but I set my priorities early. Swaying gently in my Aunt Jerry's hammock, I devoured book after book from her rich library of shameless romance novels. Tales of pirates torn between kidnapped beauties of high rank and voluptuous temptresses of ill repute filled my balmy summer days. Delicious daydreams of sheiks and camels and faraway lands eased my way into sleep each of the love-barren nights of my youth. I was hot on the trail of my knight in shining armor and no commoner would do.

Don't get the idea that my quest for love caused me to settle for the first pair of well-filled Levi's that came my way. I was certainly no nun and lived fully the carefree days of the 60s and 70s, glorious years that came after the pill and before STDs. But the romantic adventure tales that filled the long summer afternoons at my aunt's lake house had pervaded my psyche, and my soul whispered that I would find Prince Charming in a place far more exotic than Kansas.

I didn't wait for him to come to me. I set out to find him. Over the continents I roamed, meeting up with fellow travelers, living through wild adventures; always parting like gypsies at the fork in the road. Was I lonely sometimes? Absolutely yes.

Did I listen to my mother, give up my life on the road, and return to the suburbs to find a man and settle down? Absolutely not. I was convinced that the only way I would find the love of my life was to live the life I loved.

Then one day, wholly unexpected, in a tiny pension in Guatemala City called El Chalet Suizo, there he was, seated at the next table, laughing and talking just a bit too loud in a vaguely familiar northern European accent.

"Who is that arrogant German?" I asked myself while still admiring his full lion's mane of light chestnut waves, golden tan, and sky-blue eyes.

My girlfriend, Judith, always attracting the handsome native men with her blond tresses and china doll face, had already hooked up with her Don Juan with plans for a wine and cheese party. As diners paired off, the tall Nordic and I were left standing like the last two choices in a Saturday afternoon dance class.

Not having anything against Germans (well, maybe a little), I was relieved to learn his accent was Danish. No one has anything bad to say about Danes. They never have to apologize about their history. This was long before militant Islam loomed scary on the horizon and no one but Scandinavians ever read a Danish newspaper, much less looked at their cartoons.

Daydreams of Vikings began dancing in my head. I envisioned a helmet with giant horns and a broad leather vest with golden sunbursts across the pectorals. I wouldn't resist being kidnapped by this cleaned-up version of Eric the Red. He had all his teeth, smelled fresh from a shower, and spoke excellent English.

Five wonderful days later, we exchanged our parents' addresses on separate continents, his Mexico City phone number, and parted. He boarded a bus going north and I set off towards the south with Judith. No email, no cell phone. You came, you saw, you left.

I couldn't get him out of my head. While lounging under the lush canopy of a Costa Rican rainforest, swilling an ice cold cerveza, I posed the question to Judith.

"Is he the one?"

Without hesitation, she answered, "Oh yes, he is the one."

"Then I have to go to Mexico."

And so a choice was made that changed my life. Sometimes the gods truly smile on us. A seventy-five foot ketch with magnificent white sails plied its regal way into Golfito Bay. Word quickly spread that the ship had come through the Panama Canal and was homebound for Sausalito.

I had asked truck drivers for rides, why not a sea captain? I cajoled a local fisherman to paddle me out to the ship in his dugout canoe. Never having been at sea, I balanced in the rocking boat and, drawing on my literature-based maritime vocabulary, hands cupped around my mouth, bravely called out "Ahoy!"

Three wind-tussled heads with astonished faces appeared over the railing. After a quick exchange, I was invited on board and scrambled up the shaky rope ladder over the side—my first time ever to stand on the deck of a ship that was not in a museum.

"Do you have any sailing experience?"

With bravado I answered, "Sure!" The luck of the Irish in my genes, the captain agreed to give me a chance until Punta Arenas, a port forty-eight hours by sea. I was first up and last to sleep. I cooked; I scrubbed; I kept quiet and smiled a lot. I needed this ride. I was on a mission to get my man. In Punta Arenas I officially joined the crew and was on my way to Acapulco, the nearest port to Mexico City.

Moored at the Acapulco Yacht Club, I asked for the pay phone. Repeating my memorized Spanish phrases over and over in my head, holding in one hand the paper with his phone number, I nervously dialed with the other. The phone rang its strange foreign ring and a female answered, thankfully, in English. "Never heard of Jesper Nielsen; don't know anything about him. Was I sure I had the right number?"

How could I have been so fooled? How could I have been such a fool?

Two months later my mother called me in the Bay Area. "You got a postcard from South America. There's no name." It says, "Where in the world are you? Wherever you are, I'll come by."

I knew in a heartbeat. I rifled through my papers and unfolded the crumpled Danish address. I fired off a postcard with the brief message: "In Redwood City, building sailboats. Here is my work number." I did sign the card.

Ah, the poets say that the path of true love never runs smooth. Just days later the boatyard closed, bankrupt. Down the peninsula I moved to friends in Los Gatos. Not realizing the speed at which Fate was working, I was slow to tell anyone where I was. Late one night the phone rang for me. It was the mother of a fellow crewman. She got my number from someone who had it from someone.

"Sandra, where are you? There's this Danish man looking for you. He's been here for days. He's leaving the country tomorrow. He has a wonderful warm voice. You should grab this guy."

Grabbing him was my very intention. After welcoming him most warmly, I put it on the table. "Why are you here? What are your intentions?" Nonplussed, obviously having thought it through, he replied, "Come to Mexico City."

Not a millisecond passed before I accepted. Neither of us had any money. I had to work to buy the ticket.

Just before New Year 1974, nine months after we first met at the Chalet Suizo, I arrived at Mexico City International airport with two suitcases. We had been together a total of only ten days, five in Guatemala and five in California, sharing no photographs and certainly no Facebook. It occurred to me that I might not recognize him. He had similar doubts.

The first day gave way to the second, the first year to the next, and the first decade to the third and now, thirty-six years later, we are still together. We certainly recognized each other that day—not only in the airport, but across thousands of miles. Is it a blessing to find true love? You bet, but like every opportunity, luck only brings it within your reach. Your choice is to seize it in both hands and hang on for the ride.

Staying in love and staying with your love doesn't just happen. Every day you make the choice to compromise a little, to say "yes" when you want to say "no." Not all the time, but often enough that both of you feel like you are getting what you need in life and from each other.

I made a choice that I wanted to live my life with this man. In the first half of our marriage, I followed his career around the world, finding opportunities for my personal growth where I could. They were always there. When I wanted to return home, to my country, to fulfill my ambitions, he said, "Yes." Thank you, progressive Scandinavia, for a culture that expects women to "realize themselves" and expects men to expect it of them.

I am often asked the secret to our marriage. It's no secret that good friends like to laugh, companions like to talk, and lovers like to love. It is helpful if you choose to smile, if you choose to listen, and if you choose to remember the good times, and not the hard times, when he reaches for you. Indeed, if you choose to remind yourself how lucky you are he still reaches.

About the Author

Born in Kansas City, Sandra is a baby boomer who escaped the Plains on a one-way ticket to Iceland to explore the world while her friends were partying at college. She returned to the United States after twenty-five years in Europe, Africa, Central America, and the Middle East, with an art degree and speaking five languages. Life-phase three included a daughter and son, a successful scientific company, a stint as elected official and planning commissioner, a beach house in California, and always, a loving and supportive husband. The latest era began in Las Vegas with the creation of www.sandraoffthestrip.com, a magazine blog dedicated to the adventures of an eclectic mind. Just finishing her first book, *Sex and the Zen of Shopping*, Sandra is also compiling a cookbook of the best recipes from talented friends around the globe.

Sandra Gore Nielsen can be contacted at:
sandragorenielsen@gmail.com
www.sexandthezenofshopping.com

Inspiration

If you limit your choices only to what seems possible or reasonable, you disconnect yourself from what you truly want, and all that is left is compromise.

—Robert Fritz

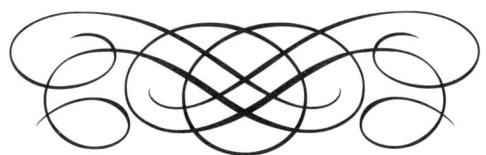

The Mystical Hand Of Freedom
CATTEL

In Boynton Canyon just outside of Sedona, Arizona, the early spring sunset seemed to hang, suspended in midair for the longest time. It was as if we were in a time warp in some other dimension. Yet the experience impressed upon me from that sacred place has stayed with me. So many years later, as I remember the events, I count my pennies and five dollar bills with a special reverence, appreciating and honoring my many freedoms each time I touch Lincoln money.

By the end of this, I hope you will look with a new appreciation at the Lincoln penny and bill, recognizing its true value each time you touch or spend one.

It was late March several years ago when a gentleman friend and I went to Sedona, Arizona. We were on an exploratory trip; half wondering what all the hullabaloo was and half-hoping for some special life-altering experience. I can say that our intuitive guidance was working overtime for us that early spring day. As the sun was beginning to paint the sky with one of those breathtaking Arizona sunset visions that only happen in the southwestern sky, we began.

We were both impressed, intuitively, to gather some things from our vehicle. We took designer water, smudging sticks (for fire), matches, special crystals (earth), and a feather (air), along with our battery-operated tape recorder. Except for the recorder to document our next two-and-a-half hours or so, we realized we had been 'impressed' to take the four elements of fire, earth, air, and water.

This is how I recorded it and remembered it …

As we enter Boynton Canyon, we see a beautiful medicine wheel right at the beginning. It is made with stones, and some sort of white powder on the ground. It is about twenty feet wide, a simple circle with a cross in the center pointing to the four directions of north, south, east, and west. We seem inspired to perform a ritual here. It is a beautiful spontaneous dance, one we seem to know the steps to—almost as if we had done it a thousand times.

Yet, how can this be? This is our first trip together, and we have never before seen a medicine wheel together. Nor have either one of us ever seen one this size.

Our steps are synchronized and we just happen to have the four elemental tools equally divided between us. The thing that strikes me so strongly is how simple, yet powerful the choreography of our movements are through this wheel. It seems as if we are being given instructions. I know exactly what to do, even though this is a brand new experience we are creating as we go. Using all of our elemental tools, several people stop to watch us, as if they sense the reverence of this sacred event unfolding through us.

Now that we have executed what I can only call a loving embrace of the wheel's and earth's energy, we are compelled to walk deeper into the canyon. My inner voice tells me there are seven wheels total that we are to experience.

We alternate leading the exploration of the next six wheels; he does one, I the one after that, and so on. (Later, I read in a book that this is a male-female vortex, with alternating and balancing masculine and feminine energies.) As we move farther into the canyon, we sense the vibrations growing stronger. The power seems to build like a static charge of energy. I feel power growing in me and become physically stronger. It is fascinating to be receiving ongoing intuition. It's like I am listening to instructions.

My inner tutor (intuition) is really giving powerful information. It seems as if we are on a prearranged mission and both of us are following the promptings in our souls; we are in perfect harmony with each other's movements at each stage of this sacred journey.

Life Choices: Navigating Difficult Paths

We wait for each other to finish a wheel and seem to sense moments before one of us is done working the current wheel. I call this earthworks; a type of ritual that seems to bless both the earth and the people doing the work.

The sunset seems to be waiting on us, as if it is setting its rhythm to our pace. I stop again to face fully toward it to absorb the energy of the sun's rays into my being and chakras. I am like a sponge; my eyes, like an energy feed to my soul; with open eyes and arms stretched out open I soak in the magnificent flaming hues the sky is spilling on to me. In the wind, I can almost sense the sound of the sacred colors of the sunset that hangs suspended in midair.

With each wheel we are impressed to leave some small thing of value to us. We leave feathers, crystals, tobacco, coins, even water, but always something to nurture Mother Earth. These are our symbolic gifts of thanksgiving and reverence.

I am warmed by the sunset's glow radiating in and through my being, I feel as if I have never been closer to God than at this moment. In approaching the last wheel, my intuition says this wheel is mine to explore. I am thinking of the smallest denomination of money, the Lincoln penny. It seems as though a voice in my head is saying, "Don't let them take away the Lincoln money." I see in my mind's eye bright shinny pennies with Lincoln's image on them and five dollar bills with his picture on them.

The thoughts continue, as if I am getting a download of information in my mind:

Lincoln is the Great Emancipator of your people, the mind of your country. He was the archetype of freedom for your people, and still is. His freedom energy still lives on in everything with his picture on it. Your Lincoln money is like a constant suggestion of your freedom, a reminder to be free and honor the freedom of others. If you honor all forms of Lincoln money, even the person with only one penny will still remember his freedom.

The Mystical Hand Of Freedom

Once again I stop for a moment to absorb the energy of the sunset and wonder how long it can possibly last. It seems like two hours of brilliance and I am still 200-300 paces from the last wheel. I see something glistening in the sun, calling to me. The closer I get to the wheel the more I feel it is a gift for me from the land. I think of all the gifts we have given and received; it seems as if my inner voice wants me to take this shiny object as a reminder of this exploration. This final wheel of energy and life.

As I approach this last wheel, my eyes are locked on the shiny object and shivers are starting up my spine. I get close enough to make it out. It is a bright shiny new Lincoln penny. I pick it up with a new reverence. This is a physical symbol of our freedom.

How many of these do we throw away? How many do we let lie on the ground, too small to bother picking up? How many of our personal freedoms do we let slip through our fingers? How many symbols of freedom do we ignore or let go of?

As we begin the trek down to our vehicle and are driving out of the canyon, the sun is finally setting. It is as if the sun has waited for us to finish our magical journey. I think this has been the longest sunset I have ever experienced and most certainly it has been one of the most profound and intense.

~

Now over fifteen years later, that early spring day in Sedona, Arizona is always close to my soul when I handle Lincoln money. I always am reminded of where I discovered my personal symbol for freedom, Lincoln money.

I choose to remember and stay aware of the grand penny and its symbol of freedom to us all. Each time I spend a penny or leave one on top of a 15 percent tip, I am saying silently, and sometimes audibly to the person, "Remember your freedom; don't give it up for anything!"

We always have choices. Do we imprison ourselves, creating shackles around our heart, mind, or bodies? What we do with our choices can lead to freedom or imprisonments. Whether we are speaking of political freedoms, attitudinal freedoms, physical freedoms, or most importantly our spiritual freedoms, each time I give out a penny, or pay with any Lincoln money, I send a silent prayer and intention …

"I give you this today to help you remember your freedom. It is God given; never give it up for anything! Continue to make choices for freedom."

About the Author

Reverend Cattel has been involved in the field of metaphysics since she was a child, learning hypnosis about thirty years ago and practicing it for many years, in many different ways. Learning how to help people find their destiny and spiritual purpose while doing regression has been one of the most rewarding facets for her.

She currently is a full-time licensed psychic, astrologer, and hypnotherapist in Las Vegas, Nevada. She has a weekly radio show on All Talk Radio about spirituality, metaphysics, healing, and even hypnosis, called Cattel's Stardate 2100 Show.

She has an honorary doctorate of Divinity and has been a pastor of the Beacon of Light Spiritualist Church in Las Vegas, Nevada. Cattel has a foster Cambodian son, is single, and lives with one foster kitty called Dagney.

Ms. Cattel can be contacted at:
www.VegasAstrologer.com
www.alltalkradio.net

Yes, It's Cancer

VICTORIA LANE

"Yes, it's cancer." I heard those words come over the telephone on August 28, 2006.

I've always been involved in raising funds for breast cancer research. Both my aunt and younger cousin have lost their breasts to the disease, so I wanted to help in whatever way I could. Every fundraiser I saw for "the cause" I could be counted on to support. I knew there was a possibility that genetics might mean I needed to be careful, but I never really worried. I felt like I helped "the cause" so I was safe. I should have paid more attention to what the message was behind "the cause," instead of just raising money for them.

So my journey begins ...

I needed a prescription refilled so I called my doctor. I was told I wouldn't get the refill if I didn't call and schedule my annual mammogram appointment, because I was way overdue. Reluctantly I called and scheduled the appointment, all the while thinking that I *really* didn't have time for this! I got my prescription and the doctor got the mammogram.

After the mammogram, I went on my happy way without thinking another thing about it. (Remember – I was safe!) Approximately a week later, though, I received a phone call saying that I needed to come in for a couple of more images. Okay, no big deal ... right?

Once again I went in and had another mammogram, then sat in the little dressing area to wait, and wait, and then wait some more. When the radiologist finally came in, he asked me to follow him because he wanted to show me something. By this time, I had a few butterflies in my stomach, but it was still no biggie.

The doctor showed me a spot on my mammogram that looked like a dime was stuck on it or something. He proceeded to tell me that it looked like a "suspicious" calcification and he would like me to schedule a stereotactic biopsy. I scheduled the biopsy appointment and left. I got off the elevator and walked to my car, but I still wasn't *horribly* concerned. I sat in my car and called my husband to tell him how the appointment went, but was interrupted by another call coming in. It was the office I had just left asking me to come back in because they wanted to do the biopsy right then.

For those of you who don't know what a stereotactic biopsy is, I'll tell you. Imagine yourself shirtless and laying face down on a table with paddles that resemble a mammogram vise. They tell you to stay very still (yeah, like I could move if I wanted to!) The doctor then uses an instrument that looks like a vacuum cleaner attachment the size of a drinking straw with a needle on the end of it. I think they used something to numb the area, but I honestly don't recall—some things are better not remembered, like childbirth and stereotactic biopsies! The needle is inserted and guided to the suspicious area; some tissue is taken from the spot and then a little "marker" is inserted in its place. That's it. The marker is shaped like a pink ribbon (cute, isn't it?) and guides the surgeon if he has to go in to remove a tumor. By the time the procedure was completed, my husband and sons were downstairs waiting to drive me home. I'm not sure why, but I cried during the ride home.

I went through the weekend with just the smallest bit of trepidation. "Nothing bad ever happens to me" was my mantra. On August 28, 2006, exactly two months after celebrating my twenty-fifth wedding anniversary, I got the call from my doctor while I was at work. Once she said "cancer," I couldn't hear anything else she said, so I hung up on her and cried.

My coworkers (and very dear friends) circled the wagons around me and took care of me during my mini-breakdown until my husband came to get me. Miraculously, my knight in shining armor arrived with reinforcements—my two grown sons. They held me tight, let me cry, and then we left. When I got home I just lay on my bed staring out the window. My husband and sons stayed right there with me, each touching me and keeping contact. Ah, the human touch—priceless. It suddenly dawned on me that I was scaring the ones I loved most and I was not going to do that! Right then I decided it was time to stop feeling sorry for myself and find out what my next steps should be. I called my doctor, who explained that my next appointment would be with a surgeon to find out what he felt was the best surgical procedure for me. I was surprised to find out that I had an appointment on Monday and this was already Friday! Seems my doctor had been busy while I was attending my pity party. Even though I was nervous, I was glad that I wouldn't have time to dwell on things for long.

Over the weekend I asked my mother to join me at the surgeon's office so she could hear everything the doctor said and could rest assured that I wasn't holding anything back from her. I guess this would be a good time to introduce my mom, Nora. My mother is absolutely magnificent. Mom sacrificed when I was young so I could attend a private school and get a better-than-average education; too bad that fact was wasted on me when I was younger. I find now that I can appreciate everything she did when I was a bratty little girl, but back then I just thought about things I was missing out on because she had to work. She is my very best friend and would do absolutely anything in her power for me, so I felt she deserved to know what I knew and not worry that I was "hiding the horrible truth" from her. It ended up being a great idea to have her with me because things I missed, she picked up on and later we were able to discuss the things the surgeon said.

The surgeon suggested a breast-saving surgery called a 'lumpectomy.' This involves taking out only the tumor and surrounding tissue that is then sent to the lab to check for cancer cells in the margins. If the margins are clear then no additional surgery is needed. If there are cells in the margins then additional treatments will be necessary. He also explained that some of my lymph nodes would be removed to see if the cancer had spread to any other part of my body. At my age I've had my fair share of surgeries, so I really wasn't worried about the surgery, just what the results would be. I was still very anxious about everything I was about to experience.

One of the parts of the pre-op testing involved having to get an injection of dye into my body which would follow and find my lymph nodes. I met and interacted with some absolutely fantastic, compassionate, and respectful people in the medical field through all this. While I was going through this part of the journey, it meant so much to me to find people who were kind, sympathetic, and understanding because even though my physical needs were being taken care of, my emotional needs were just as important but not treatable.

The process involved injecting a needle with dye into my nipple. Having a male doctor treat me like I was being a "baby" because I had tears running down my face was very degrading, but having his assistant, another male, hold my hand and pat my shoulder made the radiologist doing the procedure virtually invisible to me. Funny how the mind works when stressed …

I remember getting helpful advice from other women who had gone through the experience I was about to face. One of the suggestions was to buy a couple of bags of frozen peas. I know it sounds pretty crazy, but the reasoning was incredible—they are a perfect moldable ice pack. Another "tip" was to keep a small pillow with me to prop up the "operation site," aka booby! Of course while getting my things together before going to the hospital I forgot to grab a pillow. Once I was under anesthesia my mother went and got a pillow for me … anything for her "little girl." I woke up to see both my mom and husband sitting in the room watching me and jumping as soon as they saw my eyes open. The pain was not as bad as I expected, but I soon found out why; I was injected with extra pain-numbing medicine before stitching me up. What immediately bothered me the most were the staples in my armpit. When the surgeon took the lymph nodes out he took them from under my arm, and then stapled it shut ... it reminded me of Frankenstein!

The first day home was a bit of a blur. I seem to recall rotating bags of peas, loving my little pillow, and my husband waking me up to give me pain pills; so all-in-all it was really a pretty good day! All of my loved ones kept checking on me between my times of consciousness, which was very reassuring. Again, mental health should never be overlooked when someone goes through such a traumatic experience and my family knew that. Speaking of my family and loved ones, even my dogs were laying near me to make sure I was okay. I am SO loved!

I returned to work three days after my surgery. The surgery was performed the Friday before Labor Day so I got a little bit of a break—a little extra time off without missing work. I guess I shouldn't say I returned to work at 100 percent, though, because I found I was easily fatigued the first few days back and would leave around lunch time. The welcome back was great and I could tell my co-workers were genuinely concerned about my health and made certain I didn't try to do anything that might make me strain or get tired too quickly. Sometimes they were a bit bossy, but I love them anyway!

After what seemed like weeks, which was really only about five days, I became very jumpy every time the phone rang as I waited for my lab results. Finally, I received the excellent news that there were clear margins around the tumor and none of the cancer had spread to my lymph nodes! I couldn't wait to tell my husband, but it seemed like I was weak with relief and couldn't stop my hands from shaking. After a few minutes I was able to make the call. I think I could have heard his excited whoops and hollers over the excellent news even without a phone.

So … do you think that is the end of the story? That was actually only the beginning. When people say that cancer is a journey they are exactly right. My surgery and recovery began an incredible journey that I continue on even now. The first step after the surgery was to have radiation on a Friday and walk in the American Cancer Society Making Strides against Breast Cancer event the following Saturday. I was so stoked to start making a difference in the lives of others that I wasn't going to let a little heat and mild dehydration stop me from raising funds and awareness for and about breast cancer. I firmly believe early detection saved my life.

I made it through the radiation series with only a few blisters and burns. I did learn a couple of helpful things about treating the pain and blisters, such as putting Preparation H on the blisters for cooling and taking down the swelling. One of the other things that was helpful was using a sanitary pad under the breast so the burnt skin didn't touch. Normally I would be horrified to talk about this subject, but once you have many different technicians, doctors, and radiologists feel, see, and move your breast, it makes you a lot less hung-up about the small things. Modesty goes out the window after an event like this, but that's okay because it helped me gain strength in many ways.

One of the strengths I've gained is speaking in front of people. In April of 2007, I was asked to speak at the kickoff breakfast for the ACS Making Strides against Breast Cancer. For everyone who knew me before my breast cancer diagnosis my answer would have been a no-brainer—a resounding *"No way!"* The thought of getting in front of a large group to speak would make me nauseous and break out in hives, but this was the Vickie who had been given a second chance. She wasn't going to waste it.

I got through the speech even though I was nervous. Afterwards I met many people who either shared their stories of survival or thanked me for sharing mine. This was the beginning of the new me. I knew it was time for me to start telling every woman I knew to get a mammogram. If a woman told me she couldn't afford a mammogram, I told her where she could go to get one. If a woman didn't know how to go about scheduling one, I helped her through it. I was talking to complete strangers about breast cancer and the virtues of early detection. The shy Vickie who got nervous at the thought of speaking to a stranger was now telling stories of survivors and the importance of self examination from the time breasts begin to form. I became a walking billboard for early detection, almost to the point of obsession.

I was pondering what more I could do to help find a cure and/or keep others from dying of the disease when another survivor friend and I met some women who had participated in the Three-Day walk to end cancer. Although we were intrigued, we didn't consider it a possibility for us. The thought of walking twenty miles a day for three straight days sounded like insanity! Well, wouldn't you know it; we started telling a couple of other friends about the walk and a seed was planted. It seemed like the topic of the walk kept coming up, but none of us was willing to suggest doing it. Who wanted to be the first one in the crowd to be considered crazy? Not me, that's for sure!

Life Choices: Navigating Difficult Paths

One day I was walking around in a store and I saw a book titled, *Why We Walk,* and thought ... Is this a sign? I ended up buying the book and as I looked at the pictures the experience became more and more real to me. I remember saying something to one of my friends and it just went from there; all four of us signed up for the walk within the hour. Of course, you can rest assured that as soon as we finished registering, we were asking each other what on earth we had done! None of us are spring chickens and we certainly are not jocks. My idea of exercise is getting into the pool to cool off and getting out. Walking the dog makes me tired! But once we had time to take it all in, we decided we had better get busy training.

You should have seen our first three-mile walk; we ended up calling one of the teammate's husbands to come pick us up because we couldn't make it back. We were pathetic. Now we can walk fifteen miles and still function afterwards. I've got scars from the blisters too, but hey—it's the price we pay for our obsession and we love it! The three-day sixty-mile walk is something that makes me feel very empowered to do something against a disease I had no choice in having. I will turn fifty years old three months before the walk, making me feel like I have finally done something in my half century on earth that is making a difference. (Well, that and the fact I helped raise two wonderful sons, married and stayed with a fantastic husband, made my parents proud of me ... you get the picture.) It is a double honor for me to walk in the three-day because it begins on my mother's seventieth birthday and I can't think of a better way to celebrate her life than doing something she isn't able to do. Her sister and niece are both breast cancer survivors and I am walking for us all.

I have gained some wonderful friends through this walk and overcome obstacles I never thought I would. I've also benefited from the great side effects of walking, such as better health—actually making my doctor jump like a cheerleader!—loss of weight, gaining self confidence, and raising awareness wearing our pink three-day shirts as we take our training walks all over Lee County. People often drive by beeping their horns or calling us the "Pink Ladies" and it really does make all the work worth it—what a rush!

Other subtle changes are just as powerful in my life. I spend more time with my parents. I know that they will not be around forever, but facing my mortality made me realize that I actually WANT to be around to take care of them if and when they need me. The idea of not being there to make sure they receive the care with love and understanding I could give them makes me feel as if I would have failed them. My parents did so much for me throughout my life and I plan to be around to attempt in some very small way to pay them back. I know it is impossible to ever let them know how much I truly love them, but it is my hope that they will always experience the dignity they deserve.

When I first found out about my diagnosis I cried because I was afraid my parents would have to experience losing one of their children—one of the most horrible things a person can go through. The pain I would be inflicting on them was almost more than I could bear. Thankfully, I plan to be around a long time and be here to take care of them should they need it.

My marriage is better than ever, which is definitely a nice side effect of the diagnosis! My husband and I have traveled a lot since I got the 'all clear.' We've been to Alaska, Sweden, London, and Paris in the past couple of years. The dream of traveling when we retire has been moved up greatly and we couldn't be happier! We went to the top of the Eiffel Tower and saw all of Paris; it was like a dream come true. It seems my husband fell in love with Paris. When we came back, my husband bought me a ring that resembles the Eiffel Tower. I love to tell people about the connection of the ring and Paris, since it's the most romantic story I've ever heard of or experienced. I never thought I would have romance in my life but apparently I was wrong and I love it! We decided to enjoy our lives together while we are able and couldn't be happier about it.

I remember reading something from Erma Bombeck that was written after she realized she was dying of cancer. In the story, she mentions the things that she always put off. She didn't use the special soap, always saving it for a special occasion, put off eating the dessert because she didn't want to gain weight, held on to a certain scarf because she didn't want to mess it up, and now felt it was too late to do any of those things and regretted it. I don't want to ever experience that. I want to live every day as a special occasion and never save anything until it's too late to be any good.

God has given me a mission in life and I can't thank Him enough. Although the lesson was a bumpy one to learn, I plan to become an exemplary student and ace the tests along the way. Everyone deserves a lifetime. I plan to help make sure that happens and breast cancer is eradicated.

I haven't mentioned some other very special people in my life because I wasn't sure how to tell you about them and the changes I've seen in them since my diagnosis. At the beginning I talked about how my knight in shining armor showed up with reinforcements, aka my sons. I have two sons, Randy and Ryan. My sons are twenty-six and twenty-three-year-olds with full-time jobs and special women in their lives, but they still make time to call me every day and tell me they love me. I consider this to be a very special blessing.

Everyone in my life now knows how important they are to me; I make sure of it. I love to share this story with others so they can understand the importance of my new passion.

So here are a couple of very recent examples of why I'm walking: I have a co-worker/friend who after two lumpectomy surgeries in two weeks was told she recently had to have a mastectomy; another friend is having a lumpectomy this week. After four years of hounding a friend about getting a mammogram, she did and she had to have a biopsy, but luckily it was cancer free. Another dear friend is going for a diagnostic mammogram today, because an MRI she had showed something suspicious to the doctor and she isn't even forty years old yet! This horrible disease is impacting the lives of too many people. If the impact is this great on my small circle of friends, I hate to think about how bad it is worldwide! Statistics show that every three minutes a woman in the United States is diagnosed with breast cancer, and recent events have made it very real to me. I hope you are faithful in getting your mammograms. Make the choice now to help us find a cure for breast cancer so the only pink ribbons our granddaughters have to worry about are the ones in their hair!

About the Author

Victoria (Vickie) Lane is an executive assistant to the Chief Medical Officer of a large health system in Florida where she has worked for the past eleven years.

Vickie has been married to Roger for over twenty-eight years and together they have two wonderful sons, Randy and Ryan, along with the women in their lives who are like daughters to her. With her family's loyal support, she was able to earn her associates degree in 2002. In 2004, she received her Certified Professional Secretary (CPS) certification, then continued on in 2005 to achieve her Certified Administrative Professional (CAP) certification.

On August 28, 2006, Vickie was diagnosed with breast cancer and although thankfully she is now cancer free, she continues to be an advocate for early detection and continues to show her support by helping to raise funds needed for research to hopefully put an end to the disease. Among the numerous fundraising activities she actively participates in, Vickie, along with three other teammates, is on a team to participate in the sixty-mile Three-Day Walk to end breast cancer (www.the3day.org).

Editors Note: Vickie is one of eight people who will be carrying a flag representing cancer survivors in the opening and closing ceremonies at this year's Breast Cancer 3-Day event.

Vickie Lane can be contacted at:
V_lane@comcast.net
17041 Carolyn Lane, North Fort Myers, Florida 33917
(239) 633-7679

Family

Living with integrity means: Not settling for less than what you know you deserve in your relationships. Asking for what you want and need from others. Speaking your truth, even though it might create conflict or tension. Behaving in ways that are in harmony with your personal values. Making choices based on what you believe, and not what others believe.

—Barbara DeAngelis

Detours

SANDY KASTEL

March 4, 1954, 7:30 a.m.

San Francisco, California

The corner window on the second floor of the brick building is open. Inside the bedroom, sheer white curtains sway in the cool breeze. The sound of running water in a shower is heard from behind the bathroom door, along with a woman's voice singing.

"... *Once I had a secret love that lived within the heart of me. All too soon my secret love became impatient to be free ...*"

On the floral bedspread lies a soft blue dress with a princess neckline and a pair of stockings. Resting on the vanity next to a pearl-handled brush and mirror is a bottle of perfume, a gift box with a red ribbon, an unopened card, and a strand of cultured pearls.

The shower is turned off and a shower curtain pulls back. The voice is louder now.

"... *So I told a friendly star the way that dreamers often do, just how wonderful you are and why I'm so in love with you ...*"

Tucked into the mirror's edge is a photo of a young man and woman in their twenties posed in front of a large tree. He is dressed in an Army uniform, his hat in one hand as he holds the girl tightly in his arms. She is wearing a white cotton dress with a full skirt and pumps. She is leaning in to kiss him on the cheek, turning her head ever so slightly to get the right angle for the camera.

"... *Now I shout it from the highest hill, even told the golden daffodils. At last my heart's an open door, and my secret love's no secret anymore ...*"

Her words hang in the air. The breeze dies down. For a moment the room is silent except for the curtains brushing up against the wingback chair. The wallpaper is faded and worn, but the room is fresh and fragrant as steam drifts through the bathroom door. The crash of glass on porcelain tile breaks the silence as soft sobbing fills the room, growing louder until it is muffled, gradually subsides and the room is silent once more.

The door opens wide and in walks the woman from the photo, her white robe hugged tightly around her middle with both hands. Her face is pale and her eyes glassy, staring off into space as she moves slowly but deliberately towards the dressing table, barely able to make it to the stool before her knees go weak.

She looks first at the strand of pearls, then opens the card. She looks up at her own reflection in the mirror and studies the woman looking back at her. As she wipes the tears from her cheeks her eyes focus.

"I'm not going to let you go. No matter what, I'm going to do everything in my power to keep you and protect you. I promise."

~

July 28th, 2009, 3:15 p.m.
Los Angeles, California
UCLA, Center for Health Sciences

"You have a malignant tumor in your lung," the surgeon explains. "It's two centimeters. I believe we can go in and get it out with surgery."

Mom and I flew in this morning. We had two other appointments before this one and I made sure we were on time for all of them, which is a rare occurrence in my life. You see, I've always had a tendency to run a little behind schedule. I believe it stems back to my birth. My mom told me I was breech and the doctor had to go in and turn me around before I could be born. At least he didn't use metal forceps. I hear they can cause damage. So, instead of being born a half-hour earlier, I was born a half-hour later than I was 'scheduled'; hence my constant struggle with being on time. But today we were early to all of our appointments and it was the surgeon who was running late.

After waiting two hours his assistant called us into his office. The first thing he did was shake my mom's hand.

"Sorry I'm late. The surgery ran longer than I expected."

Surgery must be a lot like delivering babies; you never know how long it's going to take!

The surgeon is a slender man with dark skin, wearing a white coat and a gentle smile. He is sincere in his manner as he tells us about the details of the operation.

"We will make a small incision to take the tumor out. I will do a biopsy on your lymph nodes when we're in there to make sure the cancer hasn't spread."

My mom's primary care physician in Golden Valley had been searching for the cause of the pain and swelling in her joints, which turned out to be a combination of rheumatoid arthritis and osteoarthritis. During a CT scan they discovered the spot on my mom's lower third lobe on her right lung by accident.

"You'll be in the hospital for three to five days and the recovery time at home will be about a month. During that time you'll need someone with you. Do you have any questions I can answer?"

His eyes turn to my mother, his potential new patient. Leaning forward in his chair, he studies her before he asks, "Are you still smoking?"

My mom answers quickly, "No. Well, not now. I'm not smoking that much. I gave it up last year for seven months, but I started up again."

I think about how many times Mom has quit smoking. She quit whenever she was pregnant. She quit for three months a few years ago when she had a bad case of bronchitis and she quit seven months last year.

Leaning back in his chair, the doctor makes a determination.

"I won't operate on you unless you quit."

No matter how many times she has quit in the past, she always starts up again. Her defense is, "It's my only vice. I don't have a man in my life and I don't drink. Besides I like it. It calms my nerves. Plus I enjoy having a cigarette when I'm playing the piano or drawing."

The doctor stands up and walks toward us. We stand in preparation to leave. He takes Mom's hands in his. "If you need any help making the decision to quit, please, let me make it for you."

He turns to look at both of us.

"Anything I can do to help, just let me know."

We leave the office and walk to the elevator. My mother looks down the hallway avoiding my eyes. The silence on the ride down is broken by the ding as we arrive at the lobby floor.

Walking out the front door of the building, my mother inhales loudly, looks around and spots a bench beside the building where people are sitting and having a smoke, laughing and talking, the perfect social setting for my mom. I know what she is thinking before she says it.

"I'm going to go have a cigarette while you get the car. Is that alright with you?"

She looks up into my eyes and smiles sweetly. I know it's not my decision to make.

"Sure, I'll go get the car. Relax and take your time."

My mom reaches over and gives me a kiss on the cheek.

"I love you, dear."

"I know, Mom. I love you, too."

~

September 3, 2009

Ronald Reagan Medical Center, UCLA

Los Angeles, California

My name is called on the outdoor speaker. As I push through the double glass doors and hurry to the front of the waiting room I see the surgeon casually leaning against the wall talking with the woman behind the desk. He approaches me with a smile on his face.

"The operation went well. There were no signs of spreading, but just in case I took samples from her lymph nodes and we should get the results back within a few days."

An overwhelming sense of relief washes over me.

"Thank you, and thank God. When can we see her?"

"She's in recovery now. They will let you know as soon as you can see her."

I thank him again and rush out of the waiting room as my sister Linda rushes toward me from across the courtyard. I tell her the news and we hug one another. We take time to make a few phone calls and share the good news, especially to my other sister, Crystal, who went home to her husband and daughter, and then we wait. And while we wait, we reminisce.

~

June 6th, 1959, 8:00 a.m.

Mesquite, Texas

It's already 80 degrees outside and the humidity is so high the swamp coolers are struggling to cool the homes in the neighborhood.

My mom, sister, and I are getting ready for our first vacation to visit our cousins in San Francisco, where I was born.

"Are you girls ready to go?"

"I'm helping Linda get dressed."

It's always been my responsibility to take care of my little sister, but right now she doesn't like the way I'm pulling her top over her head.

"Ow, that hurts."

She pushes my hands away.

"Let me do it."

"Okay, but you better hurry up. Mom's ready to go."

I buffed and polished the floors the night before and washed the dishes this morning after breakfast.

"Hurry up in there."

My dad likes a clean house. He tests the top of the cabinets with a white glove. If he finds dirt he makes me clean it again.

"We need to get going."

Mom works as a meat wrapper during the day, so when I come home from school I do my chores before I go out to play with the other kids in the neighborhood.

"You'd better hurry up. It's going to take you at least twelve hours to get there if you don't waste any time," my dad calls out. He's got engine parts spread out all over the kitchen table again. Mom doesn't like it, but at least he's using the newspaper to protect the table.

"Yes, Dick, I'll be right out."

My dad is a musician. He plays saxophone with big bands. He lets us go to rehearsals with him and listen. Sometimes he yells at us if we get too noisy while he's practicing. We have to be really careful when we're near his instruments, so we don't knock them down.

"Alright, I'm ready."

Dad isn't going on vacation with us. He probably has to work. Plus he has to take care of our animals. We have a dog, Rover, a cat Shadow, twelve chickens, one rooster, two ducks, and a green turtle.

"Girls? Come on, let's go!"

"Coming,"

This is the first long trip in our brand new 4 door, '59 crown sapphire blue Chevrolet Biscayne. Dad already told Linda and me to be careful not to get our shoes on the white and blue leather.

"Remember to mind your mom!"

Finally, we're ready to go. We have a cooler in the front floorboard with apples, oranges, and peanut butter and jelly sandwiches. We're excited because we know we're going to play games and sing songs on the road and stop along the way to see the sights. As Mom starts the engine we turn and wave to dad.

"Bye."

"Bye."

He looks sad as we pull out of the driveway. We think we're just going for vacation, but Mom knows we're going to pick up Dad's divorce papers from his ex-wife.

~

September 3rd, 2009, 6:30 p.m.

Waiting Room

"Sandy, they're calling our name. We can go see Mom now."

We take the elevator up to the seventh floor. We have to go to the recovery room and push the button outside the double doors.

"Only one at a time," says the woman's voice on the other side of the speaker.

Linda tells me to go first.

There is a beep and the double door opens automatically. The male nurse behind the desk points to my right. I hear the sounds of machines beeping, pumps pulsing, and air being pushed through hoses. The curtains are pulled shut on three out of the four stations I pass. Mom is at the end of the row on the right.

A portable computer is set up on a stand with wires bundled and tied to the legs. As I walk around the curtain I see my mom lying on the bed. She is pale and her head is turned away from me. Tears well up in my throat, but I hold them back. I walk slowly up by her side. She turns her head, opens her eyes slightly, and smiles weakly.

"Hi, Sandy."

I lean in as close as I can and put my hand on her arm, careful not to touch her IV.

"Hi, Mom; how are you feeling?"

"Fine. Did he get the spot?"

"Yes, he said the surgery went well and you did great."

"I'm hungry."

I laugh.

"Well, that's a good sign. I'm sure you'll be able to get something to eat soon."

"Where's Linda?"

"She's right outside the door."

"Did Crystal go home?"

"Yes, she asked us if it was alright. We told her the important thing is that we were all got together before you went in for surgery."

"It was great singing with you girls."

"I'm surprised they didn't kick us out!"

"Does Chloe Rose miss her mom?"

"Yes, I don't think Crystal's ever been away from her. All she talked about was her dad not knowing how to braid her hair."

"Well, it's good Crystal went home to take care of her."

"You look good, Mom. The doctor said you really did well in the surgery."

"I love you, Sandy."

"I love you, too. I'm going to go and let Linda come in, okay?"

Leaving the room I feel a weight has been lifted off my shoulders. As Linda passes me in the hallway I tell her to take her time.

Walking across the hall to the family room, I sink into the big sofa against the window. A feeling that everything is going to be alright comes over me as I soak up the warmth from the sun's last rays, close my eyes, and let my thoughts drift back to another time when a young woman made a decision that would change her life and mine forever.

~

March 5th, 1954, 9:30 a.m.
San Francisco, California

It was the year Joe DiMaggio married Marilyn Monroe, *'I Left my Heart in San Francisco'* was written, and *'There's No Business Like Show Business'* was released. It was only yesterday when my mother got the news she was pregnant.

"This time will be different," she vowed to herself, as she wrapped her arms around her belly. My dad had been drafted into the Army. Because he's a musician, he was able to play in the Army Band. This would be their last weekend together before he left for Washington, D.C. She wanted everything to be just right when he came home. It was the second time she had become pregnant with his child. A year earlier when she found out she was pregnant, he convinced her to give the baby up for adoption. He was separated from his wife, but still married and he already had two boys. It's not what she wanted, but she went along with it. When it was time to have the baby, she told the doctor she had changed her mind. The doctor said she had to go through with the adoption. It broke her heart, but there was nothing she could do about it. This time would be different.

"Honey, I'm home."

When he walked in the door, he looked handsome in his uniform as he swept her off her feet and swung her around in a circle.

"I have something to tell you, Dick."

He put her down and saw the serious look on her face.

"I'm pregnant."

His eyes lit up.

"Really? That's great! But what are you going to do? I won't be able to send you any money. You know all of my checks go directly to Jackie. She's still legally my wife and won't give me a divorce."

"I will figure it out. Maybe I can stay with Dixie and Glen for awhile until I can find another job."

"Do you think they'll be okay with it?"

"I think so. They know you're trying to get a divorce."

"I won't be here to help. You'll be on your own."

"I know, but that's alright. I've got my family. Besides, you'll write, won't you?"

"Of course. I'll send for you as soon as I can."

"So, it's settled."

Springtime is traditionally one of the most inviting times of the year in San Francisco. This weekend was even more special. They went for a picnic in the park, spent hours talking, laughing, and making plans for their future together. When Monday came she kissed him good-bye at the airport and watched him board the plane.

She went home to pack. When she locked the door behind her and turned around she looked up and down the street wondering which way to go. If she went right, she could enjoy a leisurely walk; if she went left the view wouldn't be as pleasant, but she could get settled in a lot sooner. Looking down at her suitcase, she decided to go north to her mother's apartment.

She stayed with her mom and stepfather for a few weeks and then went to the Salvation Army, where they told her about the Crittendon Home for Unwed Mothers. Mom lived there for the duration of her pregnancy. The women at the home were wonderful to the girls, taking them on field trips to museums, gardens, and nearby orchards. The girls studied typing and learned how to answer phones so they could get jobs to support themselves. When it was time for the babies to be born, the nurses showed the girls how to pin the diapers and burp their babies. When the scab from my belly button fell off, my mom thought I was coming apart. She laid me back down in the crib and ran to get the nurse. They laughed about it afterwards. When I was two weeks old, my mom and I traveled from San Francisco to Washington, D.C. to be with my dad and start our life as a family.

~

September 14th, 2009

Nashville, Tennessee

I'm standing in a sound booth, thinking of all the choices we make and how they can change the course of our lives. My mom is home now and I feel comfortable getting back to Nashville to record the new songs for my album. I know my sister is taking good care of Mom during her recovery. It's been a challenging process, but our family pulled together for my mom, including my father, who called to remind her they did one thing right; they 'created' three lovely daughters together.

Mom made some major decisions that made a huge difference in the outcome of my life. First, she chose to "keep" me, which meant I was born and she did not put me up for adoption, even though the odds were she could have ended up raising me on her own if my father had not been able to get his divorce.

The second was when she went on that trip to San Francisco to pick up Dad's divorce papers. I later found out she considered not coming back to Dad. She was happy out in San Francisco. She had family around her, her sisters, parents, and new friends who made her laugh and feel special. I could sense there was a difference in my mom out there, but she chose to go back to Mesquite to my father.

Third, she stayed with my father long enough to marry him, and move to Las Vegas. If she had not, my youngest sister, Crystal, would not have been born. We might not have come to Las Vegas. I would not have grown up with the influence of my father and the music he played with the Harry James Band.

Mom took me to Wendy Ward Charm School in Las Vegas when I was twelve. She snuck me into the audition for Vegas Beat '68 when I was fourteen, starting my 'career' in music. She worked at the *Las Vegas Review-Journal*, who sponsored me in the Miss Las Vegas Pageant, and it goes on from there.

My producer is in the control room. There are five musicians in the studio set up and ready to record. I check the levels on my headphones and adjust the height of my music stand. I remember Mom telling me about the day she found out she was pregnant with me.

"I'm not going to let you go," she said. "No matter what, I'm going to do everything in my power to keep you and protect you. I promise."

I look at the lyrics of my song once more, take a sip of water and adjust my headphones. I realize my life has been a series of decisions and choices. Some were made by me; some by others. I was given a gift many years ago and I choose to honor that gift by giving back to others. I'm enjoying the journey I'm on and wonder what lies in store for me each day as I follow my dreams.

The engineer asks if I am ready. I tell him, "Yes."

The drummer counts off the tempo and the musicians play the intro. As the music plays I sing:

"Sometimes you take a detour
It doesn't matter where or when
You don't know where you might end up
When you're coming from where you've been

Sometimes you take a detour
On the way to where you go
Wondering which way you're gonna turn
When you get to the end of the road
Life takes a detour"

About the Author

Sandy Kastel knows all about the impact of life choices. A singer and Miss Nevada title-holder in the Miss America Pageant, her life has been a series of detours, taking her on an incredible journey leading up to a career as an artist, clothing designer, singer, songwriter, publisher, producer, and playwright.

A recording artist, Sandy has released two CDs and is preparing for her third, which will include her original songs. *This Time Around*, a tribute to the American Songbook and the performers who made the songs famous, hit the radio stations in 2007. *Only In Las Vegas*, a collection of songs from her television special, *The Event*, aired nationally.

She has two upcoming books slated for 2010. *Detours* talks of choices made in her life and the self-help methods available to all of us when making life transitions. In *Miss America: What It Takes to Win the Crown*, Sandy shares her journey to the Miss America pageant, the women she met, the volunteers who donated their time to the organization, and the tools to help young women in the pursuit of their dreams. Sandy is a member of the National Association of Songwriters, the Recording Academy, and BMI. She provides her talents and continues to support the work of numerous charities: Jerry Lewis Telethon, Children's Miracle Network, Disabled Veterans, Safe Nest, Policemen, Firefighters, Public Broadcasting and Public Radio, National Hot Rod Association's DRAW, Save the Wild Horses, and the Omni-Equus Foundation.

Sandy Kastel can be contacted at:
sandy@SANDYKASTEL.com
www.SANDYKASTEL.com
www.sandykastelspeaker.com
SKS Sights and Sounds, Inc., 8900 Canyon Springs Drive
Las Vegas, Nevada 89117
(702) 240-2930

Life of Success on My Own Terms

STEPHEN A. PHILPOTT

On your road to being successful on your own terms, where do you find yourself today? Success, for most of us, probably would revolve around our careers. Your present career could be one you didn't envision. Your current career and state of mind has resulted from your choices and chance.

Your future life, which includes your career, will be a result of your choices, opportunities, and chance. Having a successful career reflects in large part how you view the world around you. It is so much easier to get up every work day and go off to a challenging and rewarding job. A rewarding job is so much more than just being well paid. Being unhappy at work is reflected in your conduct outside of work with your friends and family.

If your career is headed in a direction that doesn't please you, what are you doing about it? Are you making informed decisions to get it back on track?

Over the years, I have discovered that happy, successful people have a few basic characteristics in common.

They used common sense in decisions, were not afraid to take risks, and had a good network of talented friends and family. When I looked at my life's journey to date, I found I fell in with this group of people.

I want to share this with you so you may look within yourself and rate your current life's journey. As you will read, there were times in my life that I had no control over and I made changes to make life worth living and a career to fit my life's goal.

I was born in a small town in northern California in the early 50s. I was the second child, three years younger than my sister. My father was already hard at work trying to build a distribution business that he had formed with his life-long friend. After my birth, my mother went back to work at the telephone company to help make ends meet. We all lived with my maternal grandmother. This strong little woman whom I lovingly called "Granny," influenced much of my early life. My earliest memories of her were of someone who could cook, clean, garden, tell stories of the past, be soft in love and stern when you crossed the line. She was always working at something. I remember going to the laundry where she worked and feeling the hot, humid air of the environment.

It's ironic the things and places you remember about your early childhood. Take a minute and think about the first time you met some special person in your life. Remember a particular occasion, the time of day, or maybe the place. We tend to forget good memories too easily and dwell on the bad ones.

My grandmother saw that I was always given something to do. Whether it was being with her in the kitchen while she prepared meals or watching her fix a plugged-up sink, it seemed like there was nothing she would not try. My father had the same drive. If anything on the car or truck needed to be fixed or replaced, he did it, and I was there to help, though I probably got in the way most of the time. With this natural curiosity to see how things worked, I started taking apart alarm clocks, radios, and even door locks to the dismay of my parents. Eventually, they found I could put them back to working order, though I have to be honest, the clocks never seemed to keep the right time again.

My mother was able to quit her job and stay-at-home when my sister entered grade school. My sister and I were quite fortunate to have a mother who focused on our every need and want. Though we didn't have much money at this time, it seemed, through my young eyes, that we had everything we needed. The thing I didn't realize was that my father was not home much. The business came first. The most I would see my father was when we would stop by the little small original store and I would run around the aisles looking at all the funny mechanical parts my father sold. At that time, I saw myself working in the store and selling these funny-looking things that I had no idea what they did.

Life Choices: Navigating Difficult Paths

Because my birthday fell in December, I started school when I was six. I was basically a year older than most of my classmates. Years in the future, this age difference paid off for me. I tended to be more mature than my peers. I was taller than most of the other boys, so I got elected or picked as class president or leader most of the time. I also chose to take on the challenge to be a leader, though actually learning to be a leader came later. I made mistakes that made me think twice sometimes. I started to question why I should stick my neck out for others.

Deep down I enjoyed the limelight when things went right and learned through experience to minimize the chance of failure. I even worked on a political campaign of a neighbor, even though I was only thirteen at the time. The new experience was everything. I would try things to see if I had any skill or talent that I might build on.

The family business started to thrive and my father saw an opportunity to open an operation in Las Vegas, Nevada, in the late '50s. The next thing I knew, we were on a Greyhound bus on our way to Las Vegas to join my father who had moved there six months earlier. My grandmother moved with us and made a new life for herself also. We lived the first four years together in a small duplex. My parents bought their first and only house in 1963. I finally had my own room.

Life was uneventful for the next six to eight years. I continued to see very little of my father because of his work schedule. I did well in school, especially in the sciences. I focused on a few close friends and stayed away from most school functions. The Vietnam War was the center of attention and being of draft age my junior year of high school, I was fearful for my future. My parents were even considering sending me to Canada, but that decision was never needed.

After graduating from high school, I decided to delay college to see what might happen with the war. I was leaning toward an education in medical research or something in the sciences. In the meantime, I went to work at the family business. My duties were just what any entry-level employee would do; sweep floors, stock shelves, and clean bathrooms. That fall things started to change. Both my father and I caught chest colds. After ten days I was over it; my father was not. After a couple of months, my father was finally persuaded to see a doctor, probably the first one he had seen in twenty years. After an examination and a chest x-ray, it was determined he had some type of lung cancer. The doctor put it bluntly; my father could stay in Las Vegas and be cut apart or try a specialist in Los Angeles. My parents went to Los Angeles, where my father started a series of radiation treatments. Unfortunately, he died a little over a year later at forty-nine years old. I was nineteen.

I had been doing some counter sales during this period and postponing my life while I helped my dad's partner run the business. During this time, I caught the manager and a couple of the other branch employees embezzling from the company. They were terminated and I became the manager. I proceeded to work all hours trying to figure out what was going on in the financial side of things and what we really did as a company. I started sleeping in the recliner in my father's old office. This went on for about six months. Everything finally came to a head; was I going to run this part of the business or sell it and go to college?

I knew the business provided most of the financial support for my mother. Though she said I could go to any college of my choice, I knew it would be tough. I had gone over the financials enough to see the company was not the most profitable at that time. I decided to stay. Within a year I had terminated the rest of the old employees. Everyone now had less seniority than me. Because there was a great difference between the California and Nevada operations, we decided to separate the entities with my mother and I becoming partners in the Nevada operation.

No going back now. There were many rumors that I was failing and it was just a matter of time until we closed.

With the continued moral support from my dad's partner, valuable help from key suppliers, and hard work from new key employees, we flourished.

I had always been interested in computers. The world of small personal computers was just developing. When the first small computer store opened near my business, I became friends with the owner. The next thing I knew I had one of the first Apple computers, as well as an Atari. Even though I was working crazy hours, I found time to learn about personal computers and telecommunications. You may remember before the Internet, there were computer bulletin board systems (BBS).

Dedicated individuals who shared knowledge on this new technology initially ran these systems. I happened to be one of these early operators of a BBS. Eventually, I was running a system out of my house that consisted of twenty phone lines. I remember the occasional question from the local phone company about my need for so many phone lines. My thought was they suspected me of running a gambling book out of my house. Instead, I became their unpaid consultant on personal computers and modems over the next few years. They finally developed their own staff of experts as telecommunications took off.

I computerized our business operation in 1976 with some of the programs that I had written. We were one of the smallest distribution firms in the nation to be fully computerized. Immediately we could make informed decisions that benefited our customers. Our costs went down and our profits soared. I opened another operation in northern Arizona. It took off and we finally added an operation in southern Utah. I attended many technology conventions and meetings with the idea of seeking out new ideas that I could adapt to my business. This kept us on the cutting edge. While some of my peers were still trying to adopt the fax machine, we were well on our way of communicating with our customers and suppliers over the internet. People continued to see us as experts in more fields related to our supply channel. We were on par with companies with thousands of employees and hundreds of branches.

During this time, I became involved with several of our industry associations. I even ended up serving on the board of directors of the largest association for several years. Suppliers brought me on their advisory councils and boards. They enjoyed my fresh approach to their mature industries. Several of these companies had me advise them on their own introduction to the internet which I had adopted well before others. Suddenly, I was the expert or the liaison between the old established business structure and modern use of technology and innovation. I was showing that a small independent distributor could have an impact nationally.

In my personal life, I continued to nurture my friendships from school and business. During the early intense years of learning the business and working late hours, I did find time to hang out with my best friend. He had returned from college in Oregon to live at home, save money, work part time, and attend UNLV. He found work as a waiter at the large Swenson's ice cream store in one of the Las Vegas hotels. He caught the eye of the general manager and was offered the manager's position at the new location in a neighborhood mall. Because one of his responsibilities was to close late at night, I would finish my work in the early evening and then help him close. I would bus tables and other simple chores, so we would have the time to talk about the day and have a few beers. I loved the free ice cream I received as payment for helping. His situation was not working out. He heard from his uncle of an opportunity to work on the Alaskan pipeline and make some great money. He decided to leave, make enough money to finish school later without having to work. Swenson's brought in a young woman as a new manager. To make a long story short, I started dating the young woman and a year later we were married. The ongoing joke, even today, is that I did not want to give up the free ice cream that I had enjoyed while my best friend worked there, so I married her. How many people can say they met their spouse in an ice cream shop? She graduated with a master's degree in accounting and formed her own business with her sister in the arts and crafts industry. Instead of having children, we both had our businesses.

My interests continued to vary. I discovered I really enjoyed cooking and pairing wines with a meal. So when I saw classes at some of the better restaurants in Las Vegas, I made it a point to attend. This opened the door to meet some great chefs. Later, I used these contacts any time I would dine at any of their locations. Friends and business associates started asking me for advice about food and wine selections. This is just another example of being recognized as an expert in a field. I found that I needed to continue to stretch my world of knowledge.

We all talk about trying this or that someday, but you know as well as I do that 'someday' never seems to come. I made the choice to make someday today. If I saw an ad for a demonstration on something of interest, I made it a point to go. In sports, I saw the local youth soccer league needed help and before long I was a coach. I learned the game along with my players. In six years, my team won the state championship in its age bracket.

One thing my father and I had in common was an interest in motor sports of all types. He had bought me a racing go-kart when I was ten and an off-road buggy when I was thirteen. This was another source of my mechanical background. Though my racing career was cut short by my father's death, I continued to be involved in racing. I worked events as an official as well as sponsoring cars, the culmination of which was limited sponsorship of NASCAR participants. To this day, I continue to enjoy attending a motor sport event.

Several years ago, my company became involved as a supplier in the FIRST robotics program at several area high schools. During the regional competition at UNLV one year, I decided to stop by at lunch one day to see what this was all about. To my amazement, I saw my company's name on several team banners and robots. This program, founded in the early '90s, is intended to bring science and engineering back into the public schools. You should not have to throw or bounce a ball to be popular in school. Being smart should also be popular. In the ensuing years, one of my teams won the world championship. Team members became interns at my company. Company employees became interested on their own. I introduced the program to the management of my suppliers and the associations of which I was a member. The expansion of this program into every school has become a new goal for me since my retirement.

Did I say retirement? Yes, I retired at the end of 2009. Early in 2007 I was poised to open a location in a new region of the country. I was well along with the program. Key employees were noted, suppliers were on board and I was within days of signing a lease on a large facility. Wanting the approval of my wife, I brought her into the decision process. She pointed out the fact that I would want to live near the new location temporarily and it would be several years before it was to the point that I would not need to be there a considerable amount of time. She had already retired, sold her business, and didn't like me being away from her.

Not really needing the additional income to change our lifestyle, was I up to the needed commitment of time and the stress to see this project through? Was it where I wanted to be in my life? The answer was no. I knew it was time to step aside and get out of the way of my management team. They were the young risktakers now. Having been involved with some great networking groups of similar companies, I knew the people who operated their companies with high standards like I had. I could have easily sold out to some large corporate entity, but I knew this would not be best for my employees or me in the long run. I approached another well run regional distributor and within a very short period, a purchase agreement was finalized. I stayed on for ninety days after the sale to help in the transition.

People have asked me if I miss the business: yes and no. Of course, I miss something that I have been involved with for almost forty years, but now I have time for many new goals and challenges. I am still available to my old company as an adviser. I have returned to giving presentations to middle school students on the importance of getting a full and valid education. As I expressed earlier, I see the robotics program in schools as an outlet for my talents and abilities. Finally, I can choose what I want to do the rest of my life with my wife and friends and not have to chase a paycheck. Though the chase I had was full of grief early in my career, I made the journey on my own terms and ended in my planned location in life.

I hope this makes you reflect and adjust your focus, if needed. Life is really very short. Choose to live it on your own terms!

About the Author

Stephen A. Philpott was born in Marysville, California in 1952. He moved with his family to Las Vegas, Nevada in 1959. He completed his high school education in 1971 and entered the family business. Because of the illness and ultimately the death of his father in January 1973, he became the president of the Bearing Belt Chain Company, turning the business around and transforming it into a market leader in the region. He sold the business and retired in December 2009. He is currently involved in consulting in logistics and technology adoption, and enjoys being involved with the FIRST robotics program in the K-12 environment. Stephen travels extensively with his wife and continues his pursuit of fine wine and food.

Stephen Philpott can be contacted at:
saphilpott@gmail.com
saphilpott.webs.com
4385 Cartegena Way, Las Vegas, Nevada 89121
(702) 376-9859

Empower

"Quality is never an accident; it is always the result of high intention, sincere effort, intelligent direction and skillful execution; it represents the wise choice of many alternatives."

—*William A. Foster*

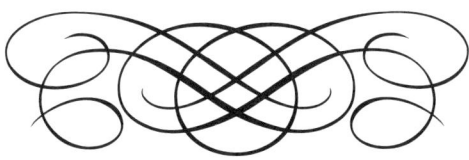

Class is a Choice

ANNE DREYER

My late grandmother was a descendant of the French Huguenots who immigrated to the Cape Colony in the late 1700s. They arrived as refugees fleeing for their religious freedom and bringing their European culture and style to South Africa.

During the depression years, Nig Lenie Bosshoff from the Boland (as she was fondly known) fell in love with and married Ben Welgemoed, my grandfather. He was a miner and they moved to the Gold Fields of South Africa in Johannesburg, also known as Egoli, which means the City of Gold. Their lack of money and my grandfather's lack of finesse were compensated for by my grandmother's example of living with class, adding style, good manners and finesse in spite of hardships. It was a choice she made!

No one would have ever thought by the way my grandmother dressed, carried herself, spoke and acted, and made each humble meal a celebration that there was a lack of money. She was simply a classy lady who instilled this not only in her husband, but her five children, who have in turn all left legacies for their children and the generations to come!

My story begins…

The year was 1958. I was holding onto the last strand of a colorful streamer, the sound of the Scottish bagpipes fading in the background as we sailed out of Cape Town Harbour on the Edinburgh Castle, a Union Castle Liner.

This was my first encounter on a mail ship, and also my first taste of travel (many to follow), sailing to Southampton Harbour on a six-thousand-mile journey to England.

You can imagine my excitement! For weeks in advance of the trip, we planned the wardrobe we were going to take. The dress code on board was mostly 'formal' for two weeks of many exciting events on board. The Captains Dinner, the Crossing of the Quarter, 'theme' evenings, and so much more!

When we arrived in London and disembarked, we were going to tour the British Isles and Europe, going back to our 'roots' which were French Huguenot, British, and Dutch.

As we were sailing, my mother explained to me about the covering on Table Mountain, a chiffon-like white mist that appears every evening covering the flat table-like top of Table Mountain. When the southerly or southeaster wind sweeps in from the southern ocean, it is deflected upward by the mountain barrier, and because moist air cools by expansion, a dense white cloud spreads over the mountain looking just like a white tablecloth. This cloth at times is strikingly visible on a perfectly clear day, as it was the day we sailed. The name was given when atmospheric marvels were published in Nuremberg, Germany in 1680 containing a picture and description with its present name 'Table cloth!'

My dad, whose hand I was holding, reminded me of my beautiful, gracious grandmother's descendants who braved three months on tiny small ships three hundred years before to sail to the Cape. After the edict of Nantes was withdrawn, these French Protestants (also known as Huguenots), immediately lost their citizenship and the practicing of their belief was prohibited. Thousands fled from France to the Protestant Netherlands. Seeing that the settlement at the Cape required extra manpower to provide for the growing demand of fresh products by the settlers and the ships of the company, the Dutch East India Company decided to send more settlers to the Cape Colony.

Two hundred Huguenot immigrants in the Cape Colony may seem a small and insignificant number, but in 1689 that was about one-sixth of the total white population in the Cape Colony. They were brave, hard working, diligent people, and most of them were highly skilled craftsmen or experienced farmers. They also brought civilization and culture, which must have had considerable impact on the settlement in the colony.

My father booked us into a family cabin in Tourist Class. My godfather, who was also our family solicitor, traveled with us to England; however, he opted to travel First Class.

This was my first encounter with 'classes,' the have's and have not's … and my brother and I were warned NOT to go beyond the barriers of Second Class. First Class was strictly forbidden!

The boat trip was an unforgettable experience and although we were a bit seasick the first few days—as the Cape is well known as 'The Cape of Storms'—we soon got our sea-legs and began to enjoy the endless activities on board; crossing the equator, being 'baptized' by King Neptune, and remembering the joy my mother and I had dressing up for the evenings events.

The ceremony of crossing the line is an initiation rite in the Royal Navy, U.S. Navy, and other navies which commemorates a sailor's first crossing of the equator. Crossing the Line ceremonies matched the initiation ceremonies of many medieval guilds, and by the 16th century, a pattern of customs had emerged in European shipping to provide a 'baptism' for all sailors aboard who have not previously crossed the equator. Neptune, the oldest sailor who had crossed the equator the most … and his retinue would come over the bows of the ship and take over the deck.

Baptism on the line, also called equatorial baptism, is an initiation ritual sometimes performed as a ship crosses the equator, involving water baptism of passengers or crew who have never crossed the equator before. The ceremony is sometimes explained as being an initiation into the court of King Neptune!

Needless to say when my godfather, who was Jewish (and therefore believed children should be allowed in adult company) invited us to his 'First Class' section of the ship for dinner and to be seated at the Captain's table, we could not contain our excitement to enter the world of the forbidden!

Twelve people were seated around the table. How smart the women looked dressed in their finery and jewels. The men, some in white dinner jackets, the Captain in a white starched jacket with impressive gold lapels, and then my godfather and our family. I fondly recall how dapper my dad looked in his dinner jacket, a memory of gracious living of years gone by.

It was here I soon realized that although we were very young, we knew how to eat and behave. I noted that the finery and jewels did not compensate for good table manners, tone of voice, or good conversation. Regardless of whether you could or could not afford to travel in the expensive First Class, status and money could not buy one *Class*.

Class is something you either acquire or choose to learn.

It is a choice!

I believe it is here that I began my quest for teaching and preaching these skills, which never become redundant and which add to our personal development: that we can choose to be *classy*! It is about etiquette, good dress, sense, and manners.

They are the elixirs of life which add to your personal wealth!

Peter

Peter grew up during the post and pre-World War years in colonial South Africa, and although there were no funds for him to get a post-matric education, he somehow had the gift, natural ability, and talent to make money.

Not only handsome (a Clark Gable look-alike) and a Fred Astaire on the dance floor … an impeccable gentleman, who fell in love with and married the beautiful orphan Ivy Swannepoel (from Dutch descent). Together, by sheer persistence and hard work, in spite of all the hardships they endured during the post-war years, they ultimately became very successful.

With all this money and success, also came the fast and flashy cars. And sadly, also the womanizing, which ultimately led to divorce, the premature death of his wife Ivy … and handsome Peter squandering all his fortune!

This was a devastating time for Peter, who by now was in his late sixties and had to console himself with the fact that he had cut his coat according to his cloth. The one luxury he allowed himself on his meager allowance was a weekly visit to his favorite coffee shop in Central Durban. There he read his newspaper and savored an espresso, which he so loved, as a treat. This went on for a number of years until Peter became very ill and was eventually confined to bed with advanced cancer.

The staff at the coffee shop he regularly visited truly missed him, and when the news came of his illness and sad condition, decided to visit him. On a Friday afternoon, they closed the 'House of Coffees' in Smith Street Central Durban, and hung a board outside the door, which read:

"Closed early, gone to Peter the Gentleman, to serve him his coffee."

All nine or so staff went to his sick bed. This was a moving experience, especially for the nursing staff and other patients. The Zulu staff from the House of Coffees sang a beautiful Zulu song in his honor and together with the management of the coffee shop, served him his favorite coffee.

The matron remarked afterward that "this was truly the most moving tribute I have ever encountered in my years of being in the nursing profession!"

Peter died the next day.

Today there is plaque in that coffee shop where Peter used to sit: "Peter the gentleman sat here."

Perhaps this true story is to remind us once again of the truth that people will not remember if you were rich or where you came from or your qualifications, but they will remember *how you made them feel.*

Peter was my beloved dad, and I have taken lessons from his legacy, which I am sure he learned from my grandmother, which I have taught my daughters, and which I strive to live by today!

Lessons from Peter the Gentleman:

Walk classy

Peter always walked tall. Although he was not tall, he had a presence as he walked into a room.

How you carry yourself goes hand in hand with self respect. Good carriage, walking with your head held high and shoulders back. Good eye contact and a smile will give you a positive self-image regardless of what's in your purse!

Read and have an inquiring mind

My grandmother, whose mother tongue was Afrikaans, encouraged her children to read good English books. On her enclosed porch, she created a small library where the Bible, Austin, Hardy, Peale, and Carnegie were read ... and then once read, we were allowed the then-forbidden novel of the time, D.H. Lawrence's, *Lady Chatterley's Lover*.

I will never forget when my father could no longer travel. He often used to say he was content not to be traveling anymore as he had become an 'armchair traveler' and would read books on all the places he wanted to visit, but was unable to.

The words of the wonderful author and theologian, C.S. Lewis, are so true: *"We read to know that we are not alone. We can learn so much and so improve our lives by learning from the life experiences of others."*

Dress Classy

The way you dress is another indication of class.

Your clothes do not have to be the most expensive or latest designer pieces, but they do have to be clean, well-maintained, and stylish. Clothes not only reflect your taste, but also your state of mind. They reflect your thoughts and your fears, and indeed precede your words.

Choose to dress smarter rather than too casual—it sets you apart. Anyone can achieve a great look on a budget by knowing quality and mixing in a few good pieces with good-looking less expensive pieces. If you're sloppy and wrinkled, it doesn't matter how much money you have, because you will look like a slob, not someone with class.

Peter always had the shiniest shoes ... and always dressed rather dapper, not frumpy!

Speak Classy

The way you speak and the tone of your voice say a great deal about you as a person, and can quickly convey class or the lack of it. Choose to speak clearly, softly, and distinctly.

My dear friend and author, Louise Richter, once remarked that "God should have made eleven commandments and the eleventh one should have read, "Thou shall not bore thy neighbor!"

We bore people if we continually talk about ourselves.

Choose not to scandal, complain, or talk yourself down. Learning to communicate well and using positive affirmations is empowering and classy.

Peter never complained; in fact, if you wanted to feel good about yourself, you would want to be with him, as he always found something about you to compliment!

Choose to improve yourself

Learn good table etiquette; good manners can be acquired at any time in your life.

Learn to be a good host and friend.

I truly believe that the summarized words of Jesus are all we need to know about how we should treat other people. When He was asked what the greatest commandment was, His reply was:

"You shall love the Lord your God with all your heart, with all your soul, and with your entire mind."

This is the first and great commandment. And there is a second like it:

"You shall love your neighbor as yourself."

The Bible, Matthew 22:36-40

You simply have to be willing to do a little work on your own. Give more than you receive and learn to develop empathy. Know your strengths and weaknesses, take advice, and make the effort!

My father respected all persons. Even in the dire apartheid years in South Africa, he taught us to treat everybody, prince or pauper, white or black, with the same respect and dignity!

Act classy

Your non-verbal message—how you behave and act—is a great give-away. *"Manners maketh man"* which is what my dad always told us!

Open doors for others, leave the bathroom towels tidy. Tidy up your mess, don't litter, and put back the supermarket cart. Give your seat up for the elder person or the pregnant lady—greet someone first!

These are the little things which add to the seeds you are sowing in order to reap a harvest. Remember: what goes around comes around!

It is a conscious decision.

A habit is something that if you continue to do eventually is no longer just a habit. It becomes what you do and who you are. So one small change at a time and adding one more over time will pay the rewards!

To become classy does not mean being a fake or putting on airs. If you truly respect yourself, care about your appearance, and communicate well, you're already acting the part.

Our actions say as much, if not more, than our words. Others can truly live and be inspired by our example which is surely our duty toward those we care for.

My dad always stood up when a lady walked into the room and yes, he also opened the car door for a lady.

Give more than you receive

Always keep *me, myself,* and *I* out of a conversation. Instead, ask *why, what, where, when*, and *how*? I believe it is in serving others that we make ourselves better people. This makes us classy.

Kindness, softness, gentleness, good manners, thoughtfulness, and respect for others; that is true class!

So it is up to you. Why not choose to become that classy person and embark on the wonderful journey of living life in the niceness of civility and class?

You can blossom where you are planted by choosing to be classy. Class is a choice, and by making these wise choices, you will reach the pinnacle of your personal and social acceptance and enjoy the good things of an abundant life!

So to end with the words of Coco Chanel, which is my dictum, my mantra:

You can be ravishing when you are twenty

Charming when you are forty

Or irresistible for the rest of your life!

About the Author

Anne Dreyer is a sought-after motivational speaker, author, and image coach who lives and teaches Coco Chanel's dictum.

With her warm and stylish personality, Anne infects her audiences as she trains and inspires them from her personal life's experience as a successful businesswoman and entrepreneur.

Nominated Business Woman of the Year 2008, Anne founded both Colourworks International, South Africa's first Makeover Salon, as well as the first Image Consultants Training Academy.

She is the founder and foreign ambassador of APICSA, the Association of Professional Image Consultants in South Africa, and a professional member of the Professional Speakers Association of South Africa.

Anne, master image consultant and etiquette expert, knows and believes that every person can blossom where they are planted and can be **irresistible** forever!

Anne Dreyer can be contacted at:
anne@annedreyer.co.za
Website www.annedreyer.co.za

The Circle of Influence: A Solution-Based Formula that Actually Works

CASEY MCNEAL

By now, you've undoubtedly heard many tales of survival, courage, strength, and perseverance. You've read stories of people who have overcome enormous suffering and gained happiness—of people who have loved and lost, and dared to love again, of those who have conquered hardships, or turned failure into success. Everywhere you turn, you can find stories of people whose strength, love, long suffering, and willpower have triumphed in the face of enormous adversity and seemingly impossible odds. Almost every *Readers Digest* cover features someone's survival story: "Capsized: How I survived two weeks in shark-infested waters with only dental floss and a stick of gum."

If you're like me, you marvel at the courage of these people and their ability to prevail against insurmountable obstacles in life; and not only survive, but somehow seem to come out better on the other side for having done so. As with many inspiring stories of survival, these stories often make you want to stand up and cheer, and shake your head in near disbelief muttering, "Why hasn't this been made into a movie of the week?" or "How could anyone have survived that, much less go on to find success and happiness?"

Before I decided to pursue my current career as a motivational speaker, author, and life coach, and even since I have done so, I, too, have had my share of life's setbacks and challenges. In my reckless younger years, I survived two stabbings, a gunshot wound, several death-defying automobile and motorcycle accidents, a fracture in my spine, and the premature death and loss of precious family members and loved ones, to name only a few of the challenges and hardships.

There were many happy times as well. I have been healthy and sickly, wealthy and broke. I have suffered the consequences of my own poor choices, in some cases making such poor choices as a young adult that I wound up penniless and living in an old broken-down car with little to eat and little to wear, suffering the lonely and destitute feelings of embarrassment and shame as I listened to the laughter of others who happened upon me while I bathed myself and washed my clothes in public restroom sinks.

The most significant hardships of my life came as a result of suffering through two separate cases of meningitis (once with a side order of encephalitis.) Meningitis is a serious and sometimes fatal illness of the central nervous system that causes inflammation in the membranes that cover the brain and spinal cord. Encephalitis causes an inflammation of the brain itself. In both cases, the pain is more excruciating than words can express.

The onset of meningitis is usually rapid (acute), and if untreated, the disease can be fatal within a very short period of time. The early symptoms are non-specific and flu-like. They are followed by more serious symptoms, which, in my case, included an extremely stiff neck, confusion, vomiting, loss of appetite, a fever of 105 degrees, and the most excruciating headache imaginable. When I went to the hospital emergency room, the attending physician misdiagnosed my illness as a "sinus problem," told me to take an antihistamine, and sent me home. After two more days of unbearable pain, some friends brought me back to hospital to be examined again. Unfortunately, I learned the hard way that a conclusive diagnosis of meningitis is made not only by observation of the clinical signs and symptoms, but almost always must be confirmed by a lumbar puncture to examine the cerebrospinal fluid, a procedure most people know as a "spinal tap." I have endured several of these painful procedures, as well as a lot of neurological follow-up examinations in the form of MRIs, CT Scans, and Electroencephalograph tests. As a result, I have suffered from chronic headaches daily for the past twenty years.

Meningitis can cause permanent damage to the brain and nervous system. In my own experience, I had difficulty regaining my ability to walk properly, a problem, fortunately, I overcame rather quickly. However, I also discovered in the aftermath that the illness exacerbated what had been a mild childhood speech impediment—it made me stutter. In times of nervousness, confusion, fatigue, stress, or frustration, I could barely get a word out.

In the aftermath, a friend recommended that I try my hand at stand-up comedy performing at an open-mic night at a local comedy club to regain self-confidence by facing my fears. It worked. I succeeded in my first performance endeavor, and was asked to return the following week to try again. I did, and again I was successful. I enjoyed the challenge, the fun, and the accolades from the audiences whenever I took my bow. I went on to pursue further endeavors at stand-up, and even attained some modest success, as I ultimately performed as an opening act for prominent comedians such as Sam Kinison, Margaret Cho, and Kevin Nealon. I performed in notable venues and comedy shows, such as *Catch a Rising Star*, *An Evening at The Improv* at the Riviera Hotel in Las Vegas, and became a finalist in the NBC *Tonight Show* Comedy Challenge with Jay Leno.

I far exceeded any expectations I had that first night when I mumbled and stuttered my way through my five-minute "set" performed at that open-mic night only two years earlier. While I still retain echoes of the speech problem, the path to my initial recovery remains clear in my mind: facing my fear by getting on stage; enjoying my successes; growing inside from the shows where I bombed; and understanding the great significance of expanding my comfort zone.

I had great adventures and met many interesting and famous people, although not always at the same time. Two of the most significant relationships of my life were born during this time of my life, which were clear stepping stones in my path to becoming a professional speaker.

My purpose in this writing is not to tell you yet another story about how adversity ends in happiness. My purpose is to share with you the formula for creating your own successes. You are also a survivor. Everyone is a potential survivor. You may have a specific story (or stories) of survival, pain, loss, or love and heartbreak, or your story may be one of general survival—the overall struggle associated with living in a troubled world, with loneliness, the search for the meaning and purpose of life, feeling overwhelmed and powerless, as though you don't live your life, instead your life lives you!

So what is different about your situation(s) from those stories of people who successfully overcame tremendous odds? The secret is found within your own thoughts, disciplines, and practices. It is not that their circumstances "became successes" while yours did not. Your personal growth does not evolve from the things that happen to you. It is developed more by the way you respond to the things that happen to you. Combine that with a daily discipline of "positive thinking" and "personal development practices" and you will reduce stress, protect your happiness, provide emotional sanctuary and life joy, and even influence the positive outcome of your life's events.

The challenges we face in life are rarely convenient. Opportunities in life are also rarely convenient. When the time for responding to these situations arises, I have found that there are three types of responses. There are people that "make things happen," people that "watch things happen," and people that stand around wondering "what happened?" You can choose the group to which you want to belong.

Your story of survival is unique, and it's a story you can write for yourself. As I have grown in my own experiences, my studies of people and psychology, whether through books or life experiences, I have found some common patterns of behavior that greatly influence the outcome of one's life experiences. I have learned that while some people just survive, others survive, revive, and then thrive.

Lucius Annaeus Seneca, a mid-first Century A.D. Roman Philosopher best summarized the components of success in these quotes:

"The bravest sight in the world is to see a great man struggling against adversity."

"Sometimes even to live is an act of courage."

The Circle Of Influence: A Solution-based Formula That Actually Works

"It is not because things are difficult that we do not dare, it is because we do not dare that things are difficult."

The most powerful of Seneca's philosophy of success is revealed through his perspective on "luck." "Luck is what happens when preparation meets opportunity."

There is a formula that you can follow to help you put these great philosphies into action, and realize greater success, more self-confidence, expanded personal comfort and overall happiness in your life. In recent years, more than ever before, scientific research has also revealed proof that our own perspectives, thoughts, and actions have much greater influence upon the outcome of our personal experience than we dared dream possible only a couple of decades ago. Of course, many motivators, optimists, and inspired thinkers have long held the belief that our thoughts can influence our success and happiness, and now science has also begun to prove it!

In reflecting back on my life, I have found that the secret to my successes in life is realized from the attitude I take, combined with the daily decisions I make, the disciplines I practice, and the relationships that I build. Whenever I have conquered adversity to win the day, I can attribute the success directly back to one or more of these practices. I have also found these practices to be common among successful people around the world and throughout history.

Here are some success formulas that you can apply immediately. By combining Positive Thinking with Positive Actions you can yield Positive Outcomes. If you practice them daily, you can learn to live your life in alignment with your desired outcomes and happiness.

I won't tell you that it will always be easy. It will take work, but I will promise you that it will be worth it! It can ultimately have the highest influence on your ability to succeed in your career, your relationships, and in life!

Positive Thinking

Where do we begin? Think about every situation in which you have ever been. They all have one thing in common. Who is always there? That's right, you. Your thoughts, your self-talk, your interaction with others, your perspective on problems, and your perspective on solutions are all generated by you. Not by the event, but rather by your response to the event, and in your predisposition of thoughts and events that have not yet happened.

Abraham Lincoln once said, "Most folks are about as happy as they make up their own minds to be."

How do you develop a positive attitude? I find that there are three kinds of people in this world, the optimist says the glass is half full, the pessimist that says the glass is half empty, then you have the third group, that group of people who look at the glass and say, "You know, I bet someone drank out of that!" You can decide what group you want to be in.

Here is a dynamic formula you can practice that will help you have more influence over your feelings, the outcomes of events in your life, and tap into the power of positive solutions. The three circles in this Venn diagram best illustrate the relationship of ways we look at situations and find solutions to events in our lives.

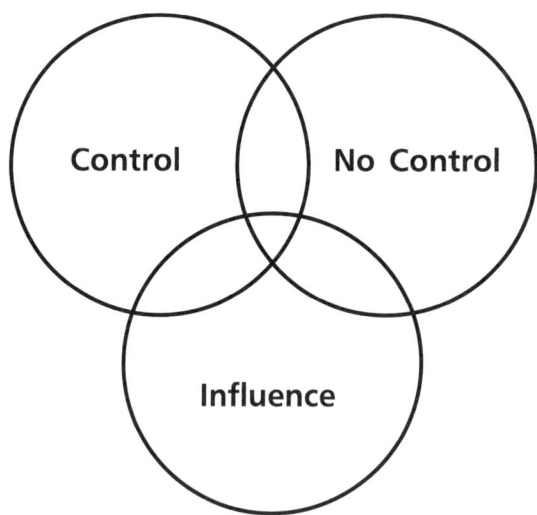

You can decide what group you want to be in.

In this world, there are things that we can control, things we can influence, and things over which we have no control. The problem is

The Circle Of Influence: A Solution-based Formula That Actually Works

many of us place way too many things in the circle of 'no control' that don't belong in there.

When I was a senior in high school, I developed a careless habit of arriving late for various events and responsibilities. My father inquired on one occasion, "Hey, why were you late today?" To which I responded, "Oh! Traffic was really bad!"

In which of the three circles was I putting my thoughts? I was definitely placing that thought response in the 'no control' circle. This further allowed me to validate in my mind that this circumstance was out of my control. Each of these circles is like a balloon. If you put air into a balloon, it expands. By placing the reason for my tardiness in the no control circle, I expanded it. In so doing, I began to train my brain to see the source of this problem as being out of my control.

When the no control balloon expands, it overshadows the other circles of control and influence, making it easier for the next problem to find its way into the circle of no control. With each circumstance you place into the no control circle, and with each thought response that places the solution in this circle, the bigger the circle gets, the more it grows, continually overshadowing the 'control' and 'influence' circles, making it easier and easier for your mind to find itself more and more helpless until you eventually get to a point in your life where you feel everything is out of your control. If you have ever felt that way, you know it is not a very happy place to be.

As you grow in your patterns of thinking, developing what scientists call your Neural Network, the brain develops a way of training itself to respond continually based on the patterns repeated previously, or by those patterns that are previously developed. Neuroscientists refer to this brain training as "Long Term Potentiation," or LTP. Simply put, the more your brain repeats the same thought response to various situations, the more apt it becomes to continually fit situations into that pattern of response. In this case, the no control response has the danger of becoming the biggest circle. Whenever a person operates too often from the no control circle, a way of thinking known as "Learned Helplessness" develops. You can actually train yourself to be a victim. Then you eventually evolve from victim to volunteer.

It may surprise you when I say that the circle of control is also not where the power lies. In the earlier example of being late, consider my ability to respond from the circle of control. Can I control the traffic? I absolutely cannot. Consider further the challenges we sometimes have when we interact with others. Can you change (control) the people you interact with on a daily basis? Nope.

The remaining circle, the circle of influence, is the place where you gain the most personal power and ability to impact your visceral and material universe.

The circle of influence is the circle that has the most power for you in life, and you will gain the most confidence and comfort when you operate from this circle. There is a formula for placing thoughts and responses into the circle of influence. You can practice responding continually from the circle of influence and trigger it with three simple words: "How can I…"

When situations come along, we need to train ourselves to look at the situation and ask, "How can I make it work out or influence the most positive outcome possibility?" How can I influence getting to work on time? Obviously, I could leave earlier, or take a different route, or prepare more the night before, and so on. We can create thoughts that encircle all kinds of possibilities for all kinds of situations. "How can I successfully implement this new project?" "How can I position myself for promotion?" "How can I finish the project on time?" "How can I influence a resolution to an interpersonal conflict?" "How can I ask the boss for a raise?" "How can I influence a desirable outcome?" Or the thought could even be, "How can I cope with what I can't control?" Even that thought is an empowered perspective. In contrast, it is natural for people to develop learned helplessness through the repetitive practice of saying, "I can't do that because …" or "I can't do this because…" and so forth. The circle of influence is a circle of opportunities.

Positive Actions

The "how" thinker gets problems solved effectively because he wastes no time with futile "ifs." —Norman Vincent Peale

The Circle Of Influence: A Solution-based Formula That Actually Works

Simply put, the thought-phrase, "How can I …" is usually followed by "… I've got an idea." This is solution-based, positive thinking. In contrast, whenever you say "I can't do it because …" it is followed by nothing. You gain no solution, no empowerment, no confidence, no benefit, and no contentment or success.

Here's another way to activate this positive solution trigger. Instead of thinking, "I can't do it because," practice saying/thinking instead, "I could do it if …" or "I could do it when …" which are both variations on the same theme.

Find the phrase that works for you so that you can practice these solution-based responses. The more you respond from the 'circle of influence,' the more it will grow, and with each circumstance you place into the circle of influence, the bigger that circle gets, the more it will grow, gradually overshadowing the circle of no control, making it easier to find yourself more empowered. With each thought response that places the solution in the circle of influence, the circle eventually gets so big it overlaps and overshadows the no control circle, until you eventually develop this as a habit for response. A habit that will lessen your stress, bring you more comfort, more confidence, more personal power, and even more successful outcomes in your life.

Memorize the phrase, "How can I…," and repeat it to yourself again and again. By doing so, when events happen in your life you can respond to them from the circle of influence. Ask yourself, "How can I make it work?" Just like a balloon, every time you do this, you will expand that circle of influence. It will continue to get bigger and bigger. Through this practice, your brain will develop the thought habit to respond to life's events in a positive way. Your positive thoughts will create positive actions that continually yield positive outcomes to your life's challenges and opportunities. When problems and challenges arise, your brain may still have an initial fear-based reaction that causes you to think, "Oh man, this is such a pain," but after you have practiced responding from the circle of influence, you will much more quickly come to the solution-based response: "Okay, how can I make this work?"

You must believe in yourself, and your ability to persevere. Winston Churchill once said, "When you're going through Hell, keep going!"

Life Choices: Navigating Difficult Paths

Positive Outcome

Visualize your success. Henry Ford once said, [paraphrased] "Whether you think you can, or you think you can't, you're probably right." In addition to this positive thought process, you must also have faith, and then back up your faith with solid work and strong effort. I learned this best from my father, Charles J. McNeal. While my father wasn't a wealthy man, he was a successful man. He was hard-working, a loving husband and father, and he was respected by all who knew him. I once asked my father what he believed was the secret to success. He paused for a moment, looked at me as if he was assessing whether or not my query was earnest. Then he looked me in the eye, placed his hand on my shoulder, and said, "You need to pray as though it all depends on God, and then work as though it all depends on you."

Whatever your religious beliefs are, I believe my father's sentiment can apply, in so much as he was trying to say that you must have faith that the universe will unfold as it should, then work as hard as you can to make sure that it does! Your hard work is also the best way to demonstrate, consecrate, and manifest your belief in your faith and yourself.

Don't try to overhaul yourself entirely overnight. Focus on the process. One day at a time, one event at a time, one thought at a time. Keep practicing the techniques, and continue to develop yourself so that you are ready when the opportunities and challenges of life present themselves. When the time for action arrives, the time for preparation is gone.

Remember that the elevator and escalator to success are out of order. You're going to have to take the stairs. One step at a time. Exercise the joys of learning, loving, laughing, and living. As Ghandi once said, "Learn as though you would live forever, live as though you would die tomorrow."

Here's to you, as you embark on the quest to expand your circle of influence. I wish you every success!

~

Portions adapted from the audio book, *Building Relationships: Effective Strategies for How to Work With People.* By Casey McNeal, PhD (produced by Sound Solutions).

About the Author

Dr. Casey McNeal is an expert in behavioral psychology, psychological profiling, and personality style type. His humorous, one-of-a-kind style has made him an internationally sought-after speaker, author, and celebrity life coach.

Known as "The People Expert," he has helped thousands worldwide achieve their personal best through public appearances, personal coaching, and numerous award-winning books and multi-media development programs, including his bestselling audio book, *Building Relationships: How to Work With People*.

Combining his notable background in stand-up comedy with his unique approach to self-development, Casey's style is both enlightening and hilarious. In addition to his popular blogging, he has been featured regularly on television and radio, including National Public Radio, the NBC *Nightly News*, and *The Tonight Show* with Jay Leno.

Casey is the founder of BrainBuilt Development Group, a Massachusetts firm that provides consulting services for individuals and businesses through workshops, instructional design and development, and personal and business coaching. His notable and diverse client list includes NASA, FedEx, Reebok, the U.S. House of Representatives and Department of Justice, Estee Lauder, Verizon Wireless, and 20th Century Fox, among others.

When not on the road inspiring others to laugh, love, live and learn, he resides in the Boston area with his wife and family.

Casey McNeal can be contacted at the following to arrange coaching services, a keynote speech, workshop, or personal appearance:

www.CaseySpeaks.com
Casey@GetCasey.com
Dr. Casey McNeal
BrainBuilt Development Group
P.O. Box 8602, Lowell, Massachusetts 01853
978-995-5900

7 Keys 2 Success

KAREN PHILLIPS

Can you imagine having a really good day, only to hear some frightening news that would change your life forever?

Have you ever gone to a doctor's appointment for a routine checkup, only to be told you need to go directly to the hospital? Now!

Did you ever get news you didn't want to hear?

I did. Twenty-six years ago. I believed I had the perfect life. I had the perfect family. Perfect husband. Two perfect kids. Even a beautiful perfect dog … a German Shepherd named Barron. I was a physical educator and health instructor in a middle school in Las Vegas. My husband was also a PE teacher and coach. My supportive parents lived in town. It was a dream life.

Then I began to have tingling feelings in my abdomen, and one day after school, I decided to go to the doctor to get a checkup. Remember … I was a health instructor, so I believed in the importance of taking care of our bodies. And I had gained new knowledge from my students' ten-minute oral reports on diseases. So when the doctor asked me what was wrong … I told him, "I think I have multiple sclerosis."

He just smiled and said, "How did you come up with that?" I told him that I had the same symptoms as those described in one of my students' health reports.

He asked me to walk toe-to-toe, checked for the level of sensitivity in my extremities, and then listened again to my concerns. With a serious look on his face, he then asked, "How did you get here?"

I said, "I drove myself from work."

"Well," he said, "you need to drive yourself across the street and check yourself into the hospital immediately and I'll meet you there by 6 p.m."

When I asked him why, he said, "I think you might have diabetes."

I told him that I couldn't go to the hospital now. I had to go home first, talk to my family, and make some arrangements, but I'd be at the hospital by 6 p.m. He agreed and said he would order the necessary tests to be run STAT.

About lunchtime the following day, another doctor came in and introduced himself as my neurologist and told me that my doctor had asked him to consult. He had me sit on the edge of the bed and ran some quick little tests. The one I recall the most was the one where he took a sharp instrument and checked for my reactions. I closed my eyes tightly. I remember hearing him ask, "Can you feel this? How about this? What about now?" My answers were "no, no, and no"… and when I opened my eyes, I could see that his testing had caused me to bleed from my feet and arms.

He must have seen that I was a little nervous now, so he told me there was a plan. Yeah! A plan always sounds good … it sounds like they know what they're doing. He said that I'd be going downstairs to have a spinal tap just as soon as the orderlies could arrive.

I asked him "Why?" He calmly told me that I either had a tumor on my brain, tumor on my spine, or MS. I asked, "What the heck happened to the diabetes diagnosis?" His response, "We ruled it out between last night and this morning."

Great! Here I was by myself in this hospital room and I had no idea what to ask the neurologist. I felt like I needed to ask something intelligent at this point. Then I remembered watching *Days of our Lives* on television. Yep! I asked the only "intelligent" question I could think of … the one I had heard them ask on the show. "If it's a tumor … is it operable?"

The doctor simply and solemnly stated, "It depends on where it's located."

That's when I realized the seriousness of my condition …

Life Choices: Navigating Difficult Paths

When I was in the hospital and they were wheeling me down to the lab for the spinal tap, my parents stopped by—just at the right time. I remember crying and quickly telling them my prognosis, "They think I have a brain tumor, a tumor on my spine, or MS."

My parents just patted my arms. My dad then calmly said, "Well, everyone's got something ... and this is your cross to bear." Mom smiled, fighting back tears, and told me I'd be just fine.

From that moment with my parents, I realized they were right. I was going to be just fine. I wasn't going to die and this was my personal trial. I just had to learn to make the best of it. I also had to realize that whatever my diagnosis was, my disease affected others in my life, too.

I believe in God, so when I received the news that I had MS, I stepped up my prayers. I talked to God and told him that I would accept this disease and everything that came with it. I said, "I'll live a good life, I'll attend church regularly, I'll put others first, etc., etc. ... *but* please let me live long enough to help my husband raise our children and please don't give me cancer, too!"

As soon as I had said that prayer, I realized what I was doing. I was trying to bargain with a much Higher Power than myself. Bargaining does not work—what does work is what I call The 7 KEYS 2 SUCCESS.

Key number one is to START EACH DAY WITH SPIRITUAL SOLACE. Instead of bargaining for different needs and wants, we need to give thanks and praise for the many blessings in our lives. We need to believe that consistency in daily prayer feels better than random prayers of desperation.

It's nice to take a moment or so to gather your thoughts for the day and get focused on what's before you. You might take time to read the Bible or a daily devotional; maybe you're a journal writer and you want to write down your private thoughts or even take time to meditate. All of us could probably make a list of things that are wrong in our lives, but if we turn those thoughts around and list everything that's right, it will make a huge difference in how we feel each day. Our problems may not change instantly, but it's amazing how our perspective will change.

The second key is to UNLOCK THE FULLNESS IN YOUR LIFE THROUGH GRATITUDE. Gratitude is your readiness to show appreciation and your act of returning kindness. It's showing your thankfulness. In my case, in addition to being thankful for my faith and my family, I am so appreciative of my doctors. I have a situation where I have multiple doctors.

When I was reassessed at the Mayo Clinic in Arizona, I received the devastating news of the formal diagnosis of secondary-progressive multiple sclerosis. That's when I was given the options for treatment … notice I didn't say cure. I could either do chemotherapy; one treatment every two to three months for two to three years or I could enter a "black-box" study. Regardless, I should continue my daily injections.

I knew about the study and that people had died of undetermined brain infections—the study had been pulled earlier. People who had been helped by the treatment petitioned on Capital Hill and were able to get the clinical trial reinstated.

The doctor said, "I guess you're worried about hair loss with the chemo treatments?" Trust me … that was not one of my big concerns. I asked him what were the biggest risks I should consider if I did this. He said, "Well … you could get leukemia or congestive heart failure." I questioned him about what percentage of the people taking chemo contracted leukemia. His answer shocked me. "A little less than one in a thousand."

WOW! I'm from Las Vegas. Those aren't great odds. If he had said one in ten thousand, I might have seriously considered it.

We came back to Vegas and I spoke with my primary doctor. It was comforting that he had reviewed the test results and had made preliminary calls to an oncologist just in case that was the route I chose. Instead, I asked him if he would support me if I could find a natural doctor to see. I promised him that I would not go to a person who would have me stand with my feet in buckets of mud and chant something and proclaim I was healed. He agreed and gave me the name of a naturopath he knew. I am blessed that they both work together—they confer, discussing possible tests and treatments to try—my health is important to them.

Now that's a big appreciation and I'm thankful daily for them. Trust me; I'm thankful for what might seem like little things: a beautiful day, rain, the shining sun, Bridgette our little dog—jumping up to sit with me—my list is endless.

The third key to success is COMMIT TO FAITH IN YOURSELF AND OTHERS. Faith is an interesting concept. It is where you believe in something that does not rest on proof. You are not able to "see" something to make a decision.

If you think about it, didn't all of us have faith ... maybe what is called "blind faith," when we were kids? When we were young, we didn't question what our parents told us. In school, the teachers were the authorities ... we didn't question them. We believed all of these people. We had faith in them.

Key number four in success is COMMUNICATION. Positive communication is a necessity to any healthy lifestyle. There are many forms of communication.

First, there is the positive self-talk that all of us need. This is so necessary on a daily basis ... sometimes even an hourly basis. I know on days when I'm not feeling strong, on days when I'm finding it more difficult to walk or see, I need to give myself pep-talks. It's real easy to have a pity-party and dwell in what we can't do or what we don't have —but reality is, it won't change anything.

When I get like this, I allow myself a ten-minute uninterrupted pity-party. One day my doctor called. My husband answered the phone and told her I'd call her back ... in ten minutes. I did just that: I made the most of my pity-party, got it out of my system, and moved on to have a great day.

I try taking my negative thoughts and turning them into positive ones. I may walk with a foot drag, but I still walk around the neighborhood with my dog. I used to walk two miles daily—now my walk consists of fourteen houses around our block where we live...with the assistance of a baby stroller for support. As I mentioned earlier, I walk with our little dog ... so people actually think that the stroller is for the dog in case she gets tired. I just let them think that as we stroll off and I repeat to myself, "I walk because I can! I'm so blessed! I walk because I can!"

When we think of communication, most of us think about the verbal interactions with others. Sometimes it's hard to communicate what we really need with others. In my case, I was used to being totally independent. Now I have to do more planning ahead, consider how much strength will be used, maybe even plan rest periods ... naps ... and I have to express these needs to other people.

This truly is a two-way street. Just as I need to learn to ask for assistance, others around me need to feel comfortable enough to be honest when they talk to me. Adults will shy away from doing things with me because they think I can't. They don't realize that I probably can do it ... just not as fast or maybe not in the same way.

I love my husband dearly. We had been talking about fun places to go for a summer vacation. He said he'd like to go to the California Adventure Theme Park outside of Disneyland. A few weeks later, I brought it up again and was ready to make plans ... suddenly he didn't want to go there. I questioned him about it, but he said he had no desire to go anymore.

I couldn't figure out why. Then I thought that he was embarrassed to go with me ... that maybe he couldn't have fun with me anymore. I called our daughter and talked to her. I wanted to find out if she thought I was off-base with my thinking about this sudden change of heart. She put the situation in perspective for me. She said, "Mom, Dad's not embarrassed to be seen with you. He just wants to protect you. Just think, you can still go and you can even rent a scooter around there. Boy, I know in Disneyland you get to go to the front of the line ... you don't have to wait as long!" Without hesitation, she saw a positive in my situation.

She made me think how to reframe my conversation with my husband. Maybe he really wanted to go, but he was afraid it would be too physically taxing on my body. She was right. He was putting off his desires to go in hopes that it would help me. As noble and kind as his intent was ... it made me feel worthless, as if my world was getting smaller.

Life Choices: Navigating Difficult Paths

Key number five is believe that EVERYTHING IN YOUR LIFE HAS A PURPOSE. I truly believe this. The good, the bad, and the ugly. Nothing we have or do is without some meaning and value.

Recently my husband and I were in Tennessee where I was the keynote speaker. The evening prior to the presentation, we went to a dinner buffet where a gentleman asked me a question while I was at the salad bar. He simply asked, "Hey lady ... you crippled in the leg?"

Not viewing myself as "crippled," I was uncertain how to answer him. I laughed and said, "Yeah ... I guess I am. I have MS. But have you met my friend Lucy (referring to my Lucite cane)?

He then laughed and said, "She's mighty pretty!" His ignorance to socially acceptable questions led me to see the truth in his question. What I had been failing to admit regarding my declining gait and strength was that it was becoming obvious even to strangers. This man was placed in my life, with his inappropriate question, to make me take action to prevent a further decline in my condition. I would thank that man today if I knew how to contact him.

SAVE YOUR ENERGY AND YOUR EMOTIONS is key number six. Anger, jealously, and self-pride can needlessly consume all of us. We need to practice forgiveness and appreciation. Save your energy for the situations that really matter.

When my children were young, they'd cry as they tattled on one another. I would ask, "What if you need those tears later? What if you use them all up right now?" As Richard Carlson says in his book, *Don't Sweat the Small Stuff*, remember, in life's big picture, it's all small stuff.

When I finally was diagnosed with MS, it was with a telephone call from my neurologist. He simply said he had the test results back and I had MS. I asked when I should come back in for an office visit. His answer shocked me, "When you become blind and/or paralyzed." Needless to say, I didn't go back to see him ... in fact, I changed doctors.

This statement has remained with me forever and when I combined this with the "crippled leg" question, along with my increased weakness, I knew I had to try and preserve what range of motion I still had in my legs.

I'm pleased to announce the new addition to our family. In addition to Lucy, my Lucite cane, her brother Blake (he's blue), and their sister Amber (she's bronzy in color), they now have a "techie sister" named Brianna. She is a computerized walking aide that straps on below my knee and electronically stimulates my nerves. It causes my ankle and leg muscles to contract and relax, thus allowing my walking gait to appear more normal. She is truly a "Brain in a Box" and she really helps me save so much energy every day.

The final key in the 7 Keys 2 Success is STAY SILENT AND STILL ... LISTEN. We must be open to outcomes. Things may not always be going the way that we think they should, but that doesn't mean they aren't in alignment with the big picture of our lives.

I can remember when I was the principal of the largest middle school in the state of Nevada with approximately 2,300 teens. It felt like we unlocked the doors in the morning, served breakfast, served lunch, and then it was the end of the school day.

We had four separate lunch schedules to accommodate all of the students and staff. One day it seemed like we had an extraordinary amount of students at lunch. I asked each adult supervising lunch what they thought. "Do we have more students in here than normal?"

After asking all of the adults, I decided to listen to my inner voice. I asked the assistant principal to go room to room in each hallway and verify that each classroom was following the assigned lunch schedule. This took two days to verify.

At the end of the second day of frustration, from what I thought were overloaded lunch periods, I went to my eye doctor appointment. To my delight, the doctor listened to my anguish. He then told me he knew what was happening ... why there seemed to be so many students at each and every lunch. I had double vision! With a pair of corrective lenses, my mystery of the overloaded lunches was solved ... but not before I apologized to all the staff that I questioned and inconvenienced during the two-day drama. I certainly learned that I needed to stay silent and still and listen; whether it's listening to my inner voice or the voices of others ... I needed to listen more.

Just as I have had to change how I view my life with MS, you may have to change your views on some things. Remember life changes: daily, constantly. A positive attitude sure makes the storms in our lives easier. Look at what you *can do* instead of what you *can't do*. A positive attitude can help reduce stress, attack your fears, and keep your passion alive.

Every day I make a decision as to what type of day I'll have. My attitude is a choice ... AND SO IS YOURS. Remember, circumstances do not define you, but your attitude and actions sure can.

Dr. Wayne Dyer once said, "If you change the way you look at things ... the things you look at change." It's one of my favorite quotes. It's worth repeating. And worth remembering. "If you change the way you look at things ... the things you look at change."

About the Author

After thirty years in the area of education, Karen Phillips has created a new life-story where she is now recognized as a keynote speaker and Christian leadership coach. She inspires her audiences to be empowered despite the challenges they may face.

Karen's educational career was in health and physical education, where she was honored through the National Teacher of the Year Program and then moved into educational administration. She is a member of the Citizens Advisory Board for the Nevada Chapter of Multiple Sclerosis and serves in a leadership role of an internationally-based women's Bible study group.

Karen married her husband, Eddie, in 1976 and together they have raised two children and have been blessed with six grandchildren. They reside in Henderson, Nevada—a suburb of Las Vegas—and enjoy family time, outdoor activities, and relaxing at their cabin in Utah with their two dogs, Bridgette and Gigi.

Karen Phillips can be contacted at:
Karen@EmpoweredPotential.com
www.empoweredpotential.com
2509 Antique Blossom Avenue
Las Vegas, Nevada 89052
(702) 269-7979

ourage

It is our choices that show what we truly are, far more than our abilities.

—*Joanne Kathleen Rowling*

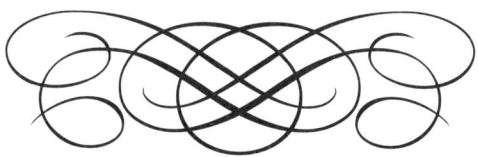

Life Forced

SUSAN HALLER

A psychic friend who knew my husband stated simply: "You have so much cancer outside your body that if you don't leave this man, you will be dead in three years and your children will watch you die."

Eighteen hours later ... the kids and I were on the road.

Two kids, $237.00 under the rug of a 1982 Honda Civic Wagon with 225,000 miles on it, two paper bags, a couple of suitcases, a couple of stuffed animals, and a whole lot of mustered courage. We were going away from the darkness of Post Traumatic Stress Syndrome and an impending brain aneurism and into the light of a new life.

I had only one thing to say to my kids. "I cannot offer you anything but an adventure. I cannot guarantee college, or a fancy house, a lot of money or beautiful clothes, but an adventure we will have and after all is said and done, you will know how to have adventures of your own. No matter what happens, you will know you can get through any drama that comes your way. Now, you have two choices; you can stay with 'Dad' or you can come with me ..."

"We're going with you, Mom!" was the resounding answer. "What took you so long?"

There is a funny truth about choices. We tend to make the very best choices we can, based upon the information we are given at the time. Mine had led me into a cloistering relationship with my second husband ... an offshoot of an abusive relationship with my first husband. Number one, I married for passion; number two, for protection. The reasons are always much deeper than a simple paragraph can describe. So many threads make up the fabric of an experience that to weave them back together is more work than memory needs to relive. Suffice it to say, it was time to move on.

While a brilliant artist, Vietnam had taken its toll on yet another veteran who, as one wise person put it, "left his body on the battlefield." Night terrors, a growing psychosis, moodiness, dark thoughts, pressure on his brain, and finally the purchase of a Kimber 45 semi-automatic to protect us from "the bad people" (Columbine had just happened), brought such a sense of unrest to the house that it was obvious we were in danger of becoming a murder/suicide family.

Was it the fact that he was meeting me at the door with a cocked and loaded pistol pointed at my head? Or was it when my beautiful seven-year old daughter said to me, "You know, Mommy, today Dad spent a couple hours polishing the bullets of his new gun. Don't you think he is getting a little paranoid?" (An appropriate description of his actions and a very grown up word for a small child.) Perhaps it was the fact that he was now seeing Viet Cong in the bushes ... of Oregon. Regardless, all signs pointed to "we're outta here!"

We had been given only one piece of advice. "Go into the shelter system; you will have a month to figure out your next move."

We went from a small town in Oregon to Seattle, where I had lived for many years. All the way up the road we were crunching loudly on potato chips (previously forbidden because it brought back the sound of battle) and shooting imaginary balloons of icky memories out the back window of the car so that they could splash on the road and get squished by huge semi trucks. We also planned to treat ourselves with concerts. My daughter chose Spice Girls, my son, Garth Brooks, and I chose Bette Midler. Having no idea if any of these entertainers were actually touring, they were our favorites at the time, and represented freedom through the music they played.

I drove up the road and into the heart of downtown Seattle, wondering just how to find a shelter to go into. My daughter, seeing folks laughing on the street corner said, "People are laughing, Mom. I didn't know people laughed in the city; I thought everybody just hurt each other." My son's observation about "life on the outside" was the number of signs telling people what to do and when to do it. "No Parking, No

Stopping, No Walking." A telling statement to the neurosis we had just abandoned. The lady at the "cheap" motel looked at us, our car full of stuff, and our eyes tired, and gave us an incredible deal on the room. I got out the phone book and started to make calls.

As often happens, psychotic people live in such fear that they close off the life of those around them and as a result, I had not seen or spoken to my family for a full five years. There was no way that we could possibly just arrive on the doorstep of relatives who may not want us around. The process of re-entry was one that could only happen in small meetings and without any exchange of needs. My daughter had never really met them and my eleven-year-old son could not really remember them. I was not even sure that we could develop any kind of relationship after all of the anger my husband had caused. Many conversations were about murdering my mother and the method for her demise. Though unsettling and strange, I had taken the gun and had it with us for our protection, if only to know that he wasn't coming our way with it.

What happened to me? The free creative spirit that brought humor and life to every situation, a singer, songwriter, theatrical personality, bigger than life "Auntie Mame" had allowed a slow dimming of my huge light to the point that driving off the road in the middle of the night had actually been a thought. Unable to face my reality, I would drive endless circles to make sure that all bodies were sleeping when I arrived home.

Where was the woman who had written children's musical comedies? Where was the woman who adored gowns and tall shoes, sassy hair and big songs? Entertaining a crowd, hearing laughter, bringing the audience to tears; warm smiles and creative songs were a passion, and that passion was now reduced to a tiny mustard seed tucked way deep inside an abandoned heart. The only thing saving me was the need to show my children that life existed … and it was truly glorious. I had only to relocate mine.

The biggest issue I faced was the fact that my kids had been homeschooled without ever really getting any formal schooling. Bad people went to school and Columbine was the direct result of what happens inside a school system. That being the case, how and where was I going to educate them? I couldn't take kids who had never sat down at a desk and put them in with 3,500 other children. How would they be able to survive?

So here I was, staring at the ceiling of a cheap motel, listening to my kids sleeping, finances reduced to $180, and living on faith that we would have enough. The shelter took us in the next day.

There is a strange, instant camaraderie that happens in women's shelters; a blue ribbon binds us all together and makes us a family for a few minutes. Bruises live next to tears, hugs are abundant with women and children we don't know as if to say, "I am here and know where you have been ... you are going to be ok." We met, we talked, we listened; we found ways to laugh and we got up the courage to move on.

I left my kids with another mother for a few hours to think alone and started driving around Seattle. Having lived there for more than thirty years, I knew directions to go and where things were located. I started early and was still driving around in late afternoon daunted by the size of the schools and the price of the neighborhoods.

"Move to Port Townsend!" the voice came right into the car ... loud and clear ... or should I say, "LOUD and CLEAR!" I immediately turned around and went back to the shelter and talked it over with the counselor.

I had lived in this wonderful Victorian town as a child and knew it well. Built in the late nineteenth century, this pristine tourist community has a thriving arts association, 500 Victorian homes, small schools, is surrounded by water and has a newspaper that comes out every Wednesday. Truly one of the most beautiful places on earth and a place I consider near and dear to my heart.

Shelters have an interestingly supportive inter-network that goes out of its way to help women and children in need. Especially women who are only "passing through"; they got us into a hotel room for a night so that we could check out the town and see if any opportunities were available. My daughter spent the time looking at the floor of the car with folded arms and a surly expression and my son was sick with an "emotional" stomach flu. The good news was the ad in the local paper that said, "singer wanted for new restaurant" with an address to a Victorian house that resided right across from a childhood home. It certainly did NOT look like a restaurant, but I knocked on the door and was greeted by a tall, artistic-looking woman holding a blonde-headed child on her hip. I spent the next ten minutes standing on her front porch regurgitating my story before allowing her to speak. I am sure she thought I was crazy.

When I finally took a breath, she sent me down to The Upstage, her husband's San Francisco-style jazz restaurant that was still in the scaffolding stage of build out and far from ready to open. In the car, one of the few possessions I had was a CD with the background music for *Aesop's Fables*, a children's musical comedy I had written many years earlier. The place had a boom box; I did my best ever Broadway-style audition and said, "Well, you gonna hire me?" The kids were back at the room and we only had the one day to get settled.

With a bewildered look on his face and compassion in his heart, he said. "Well, I guess I could put a paintbrush in your hand."

"Good, I'll be back Friday morning at 8:00!"

"Make it 10:00 … we don't start that early here."

Frankly, they took the paintbrush away after they saw the abysmal job I did in the bathroom. Apparently painting is a gentle soft motion, whereas scrubbing the grill is good for getting the ex out of your system. Scrubbing the dance floor on my hands and knees for a few days was also highly effective, along with scrubbing the exposed brick work to get out the smell of the old bar. At one point I yelled out to nobody in particular, "Oh My God, I think I feel a Spiritual coming on," to which the owner's wife leaned over the railing and said, "Well, you just go right ahead and sing it, honey!"

Sing I did! I sang loudly, softly, painfully, and joyfully. I met other artists and painters who wanted to paint portraits of me, loving the length of my neck and the shape of my nose and small breasts, dismantling the controlling mantra that my husband had filtered into my system regarding "a boob job, a nose job, and liposuction" to reshape my body and put my psyche off balance in the process.

I found voice, form, artistic abundance, and hope that dreams could return. The mustard seed of life that lay dormant waiting to be nourished was slowly sprouting. My children and I danced cautiously and carefully around family members and long distant friends. My son declared, "Get me a counselor. Get me a counselor now! I don't want to go through life with these problems." My daughter found friends and safety in her new school and we became refreshed. The Upstage made me a town celebrity and brought out the very best in my creative form and function. I learned how to breathe again.

About the Author

Founder, Owner, and Chief Creative Officer of S.H.E.—Susan Haller Enterprises—Susan Haller has over a decade of experience in fundraising and the development, marketing, and in-person sales of a wide range of creative products. Her successes have included entertainment, music, special event production, fashion, toys, fine art, and numerous advertising media including print, outdoor, on-line, and television.

Susan is a proven business manager with leadership, marketing, sales, and office operations experience in industries as diverse as retail, hospitality, live theater, travel, television production, gaming, and even high technology.

Susan has composed over two hundred original songs, four stage musicals, six children's books, thirteen network TV commercials, and countless voiceover scripts, advertisements, and media releases. She is an accomplished performer, having starred in numerous children's shows, live stage productions, and cabaret musical events, as well as in radio and TV commercials in the Seattle and Las Vegas media markets.

Susan Haller can be contacted at:
Susanhaller555@yahoo.com
7300 Pirates Cove Road #2009, Las Vegas, Nevada 89145
(702) 328-7431

New Beginnings

MARY MONAGHAN

'Three months will go quickly; I'll be back before you know it.' These were the last words my husband John said to me as he left our home in Johannesburg, South Africa for a three-month backpacking trip to Australia. It upset me to say good bye, but I knew that he needed some time and space. He had been experiencing financial problems with the company he owned and felt he needed a break before coming back to South Africa and starting afresh. Little did I know as I said goodbye that day how my life was about to change.

We had met in an Irish club in London and then had moved together to South Africa in the 1980s, getting married shortly afterwards. Our marriage was a good one, the envy of our friends who called us 'the happy couple.' We loved being together and our happiness shone through for all to see. I knew our love was so strong it could weather any storm.

While John was away I threw myself into my work. It was tough; I missed him terribly, the sound of his voice and the warmth of his hugs. I was so very lonely without him; we were a team, and I didn't function well without my partner. As time went by not only did my loneliness increase, but I was also starting to realize the extent of his money troubles as endless final demands arrived in the mail. I did the best I could to keep all the creditors at bay as I waited for his return; I just knew he would make everything all right when he got back; he always did.

The only trouble was that after three months there was still no sign of John. I had no way of contacting him in Australia; I just had to wait for him to contact me. It was before the days of cell phones and e-mail; he had to pick up the phone and call me. I had no way of getting in touch with him as he was backpacking in remote areas of the Australian bush. But how long could I wait? He had promised to come back; he loved me and had always kept his promises so I decided I just had to be patient. I was constantly stressed and nervous; what if he had had an accident, what if something terrible had happened to him? I contacted his family in Ireland; they had no news, either. I couldn't eat, I couldn't sleep, I felt helpless. My weight dropped dramatically; I looked tired and haggard. The strain was clear for all to see.

As weeks went into months I made contact with private investigators and Interpol. I needed to know what had happened to him. I knew he would be in touch with me if he was okay; something had to be terribly wrong. Despite all my efforts, I made no progress; he was nowhere to be found. My friends were as concerned as I was. John would not just disappear from my life; he wasn't like that. As months turned into years and there was still no sign of him, they tried to encourage me to move on with my life. I was still young, I needed to start afresh, meet new people. I had to accept that John had vanished and that I would probably never see him again, I had to move on. I listened to their arguments, but I couldn't do it; I wasn't ready. How could I give up on him so soon? I realized I would continue to search for him always; I needed to know what had happened. I would not rest until I had uncovered the truth behind the mystery of his disappearance.

My life had fallen apart in front of my eyes. Our beautiful home with swimming pool and guest cottages was repossessed and I moved to a tumbledown house with rotting floorboards and broken windows with no money to fix it up. I had barely enough money to buy food, surviving on cheese and crackers. Things could not get any worse, or so I thought. I was wrong; it could definitely get worse.

Three years after John had disappeared, one of his friends finally broke the news to me of John's infidelity, a secret he had kept from me all this time. This revelation coming so long after John's absence put a totally new light on things. Sad and angry I realized that I could no longer wait for John to come back; he was probably never coming back. It was now up to me to make a new life on my own. It had taken years, but now my eyes had been opened, it was time for me to reclaim my life.

New Beginnings

As that realization came to me, I felt my shoulders move back, my back straighten; I was no longer forced to carry the weight of the world on my shoulders. I could discard it; it was my choice. I was not going to be the victim in all of this any more. I was going to take control of my life. It was time for new beginnings. I had been waiting for so long for someone else to solve all my problems, but it was now up to me. It was a scary thought but a liberating one, too. I wasn't stupid; I could become creative and find ways to make money. I just had to have the will to do it.

I picked myself up and started doing things which were totally out of character, but necessary in order to get by. In addition to my job at American Express, I bought some chickens, and became a chicken farmer, selling eggs at work to make some extra money. Little by little, I managed to scrape enough money together to get my life back on track. Each bit of progress was notched up as a small victory for the new me, Mary the survivor.

I knew I would never fully manage to start afresh without freeing myself of John, but as an Irish Catholic I grappled with the idea of divorce. With time I came to the realization that I could spend the rest of my life living as a married woman, not even sure if I was a deserted wife or a widow; I would never know if John was alive or dead. It was not right for me to put my life permanently on hold; I needed to be open to the possibility of new relationships. So after much soul-searching, I decided to go through a divorce and annulment. I knew now that I would survive what had happened; it was a terrible thing and had caused me the most incredible heartache, but I would not allow it to ruin my entire life.

Despite my decision to move on with my life, I was not going to give up on my search for John. I deserved answers to my questions and to understand why he had done what he had done, so I never stopped searching for him. As time went on, I became less and less obsessed with finding him and my emphasis shifted to making a new life for myself. I found a new job which paid a lot more money and now that I had a senior position, I could afford to move to a new house, travel, and learn to do many new things I would never have done if John was still in my

Life Choices: Navigating Difficult Paths

life. I learned to scuba dive. I took a game ranger course and travelled to Uganda and Rwanda to see the mountain gorillas. I felt like a bird that had been set free. I could do anything I wanted to; I just had to believe in myself enough to do it. I was no longer a wife, dependent on her husband. I was responsible for creating my own life and I could make of it what I wanted.

While being immensely sad and hurt at what had happened, I made a conscious choice to give John and men in general the benefit of the doubt. Yes, he had done a dreadful thing, disappearing without a trace, without telling me that he did not intend to come back. He should have let me know what was going on and then I could have moved on with my life a lot quicker. There was no doubt that it was a terrible thing, but I knew in my heart he had not done it out of malice. I refused to become bitter and twisted and wary of all men as a result of what had happened to me. They were not all out to get me, that was for sure. Condemning all men would serve no purpose and would ruin any future chance I might have of happiness. I chose to maintain a positive attitude, be open to new experiences and not let this one bad experience cloud the rest of my life.

I was now a survivor, surrounded by family and friends, living life to the fullest, travelling and experiencing new things. I knew I would eventually find John; it was just a question of time, but finding him now would be in many ways an anticlimax. I had moved on. I had grown into a different person. He no longer figured in my life.

My friends encouraged me to write a book about my experience: John's disappearance, my search for him, and the series of coincidences which eventually led me to find him. It would be an account of my very personal journey. Who would have thought I would become a writer? I wrote my book, *Remember Me?* as a way of sharing my personal growth journey and the ways I managed to survive and work through my problems. I was overwhelmed by the positive response it received, so many wonderful calls to radio shows and supportive e-mails. I realized I had done the right thing in sharing this very personal part of my life, as it helped other women in similar situations talk about their stories, too.

My life had become a series of new beginnings as a result of what had happened to me. I had grown so much and had discovered new things about myself. I found an inner strength which I did not know I had and a determination to overcome any obstacles put in my way. I had been given the choice of being overwhelmed by what had happened to me or turning it into a force for good. I chose the positive, becoming my own person with no resentment or bitterness; a new me, strong, independent, and free. I embrace my new life for its endless possibilities and the joy it continues to bring me every day.

About the Author

Mary Monaghan is the author of *Remember Me?*, a story of survival and new beginnings, now also adapted into a screenplay. She was a contributor to *Writing the Self*, an anthology of women's writing and is currently busy with her second book, *Who do you belong to?* due for publication in 2010.

She lives in Cape Town, South Africa and travels frequently to Europe and the United States. As well as being a successful writer, she is a speaker and also facilitates change and leadership development interventions. She has a passion for helping people develop themselves to be the very best they can be.

Mary Monaghan can be contacted at:
marymonaghan@telkomsa.net
www.marymonaghan.com
P. O. Box 163, Melkbosstrand 7437, South Africa
00 27 83 625 9470

Hope

Happiness and love are just a choice away.

—Leo F. Buscaglia

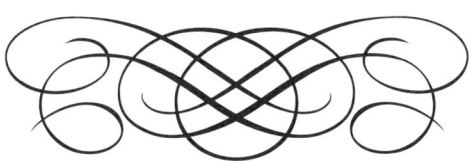

Creating My Dream Life: A Woman's Journey from Homelessness

SHERIAL BRATCHER

We make a living by what we get; we make a life by what we give.
—Sir Winston Churchill

Looking back at my life, I can see why I am so tenacious, eager to be successful, and have such a passion for making life better for myself and others. For me, life has never been as good as it is today and for that I am very grateful.

I was born in Oregon. My mother and father divorced when I was nine. Although we had a very nice home, my father was very violent and my life was full of fear and anxiety. At seven, I developed a stomach ulcer which I had until I was fourteen. My mother moved my two brothers and me to Oklahoma with a man she barely knew, and the next five years were just as painful as before. We lived with this man's family off and on in a little one-room shack, but many times we just lived in a car. Because our situation was so tenuous and we moved around so much, I attended forty-two schools. Even then, I had to miss a lot of school because my mother was sick much of the time and I had to take care of the younger children.

Between helping to raise my younger siblings and being homeless, I had nothing that even vaguely resembled a "normal" childhood. I really had no childhood at all. I spent whatever private time I had—and when cooking for my mother and brothers—daydreaming that I was cooking for my husband and children and envisioning a life far different and better than the one I was actually living. I believe that it was the daydreaming and desire for a better life that kept me from falling into total despair and hopelessness.

When we lived with this man, I had to sleep on a pull-out couch with my two brothers. We hardly had anything to eat and life became even harder, because my mother had three more children. Moving there simply continued the nightmare I had already been living. I had no friends because we moved around so much, I was embarrassed because my clothing was so ragged, and I had a lot of health issues because of the lack of food.

One very clear memory was a time when I went to a new school, I was given a pencil. It was so special to me because it was one of the few gifts I ever received and it was brand new. I really treasured that pencil ... it had an eraser that had never been used.

In 1964, my life again changed very dramatically. Things were so bad that with just the clothes on our backs, we took a five-day train ride to Canada to live with my mom's sister. Truthfully, anything was better than the situation we were living in. We now had a home, but I was still having to take care of my younger brothers. However, I was now able to be in one school and, although my home life was a bit more stable, I still longed for something better. I always had the feeling that I was looking out at a beautiful world to which I didn't belong. At the same time, I had some belief deep within myself that someway, somehow, I could build a life that would fulfill my dreams.

In August of the year I was fourteen, I met Reno, a nineteen-year-old French Canadian man who, although he could hardly speak, write, or read English, was very ambitious. He, too, was seeking a better life for himself. My grandpa always told me that the Lord was coming any day so I would pray that I could have a home and a baby before that day came. My family relationships had always been so tenuous and strained, I really wanted to create my own family.

Reno and I married on September 24, 1966. I dreamed a lot about how my new life with Reno was going to be. I thought I finally had everything I always wanted ... a husband, three beautiful children by the time I was twenty-one, and a career. Reno and I both worked very hard

Life Choices: Navigating Difficult Paths

and we had a nice home. I was working two jobs, one of them running Reno's successful logging business. I still had the time and energy to take care of my wonderful children. I was living what I thought was my "dream" life. I went back to school and got a government job working with handicapped adults. I taught nineteen people how to grocery shop and prepare food. As time went on, I kept getting promoted, became the program coordinator, and developed many other programs with an annual budget of approximately $2 million. I loved this work and I did it for more than twenty years. It was very gratifying to me to be able to help so many people in need. I certainly understood what being in need meant.

It was working there that I began to realize the depth of my intuition about peoples' needs and my compassion as well as my ability to successfully create and run various programs that could benefit others in an important way. My job now demanded that I travel, which I also loved. At the same time, I began attending various self-empowerment seminars to help me overcome my lack of self-confidence and to gain new skills, tools, and insights into both my personal and professional life. Although I kept trying to deny it, I realized I was not happy in my marriage. Reno and I had begun to grow apart and, heartbreakingly, we divorced after twenty-three years of marriage. Reno had always told me my turn would come for attention from him. However, that time never came and I felt miserable, alone, and unappreciated. My "dream" life was collapsing around me.

I remarried, but had it annulled three weeks later. I married again. Another mistake. Although he was very nice, I didn't really love him. I was always in search of a life that kept escaping me. After several unsuccessful marriages and some bad financial advice, I was bankrupt and lost everything I had managed to accumulate over the years. It was clear I had to stop making bad choices, learn from my mistakes, and attract what I was so desperately seeking.

When the World Trade Center was attacked on September 11, 2001, I just knew it was my time to come back to the U.S. On January 31, 2002, I moved to Las Vegas with just my suitcases, $600, and my will and drive to succeed. My brother lived there and, once again, I was sleeping on a pull-out couch. Somehow, I knew instinctively that Las Vegas was where I was to be. I would be successful again and be able to rebuild a new and better life for myself.

In 2004, I founded Diamond Star Networking, a business networking organization. I started it with just sixty-four members. Within two years, it had grown to four hundred members and I was delighted. With my natural gift of connecting people, and the ability to help others grow and make their dreams become reality, I received a great deal of recognition as an expert in branding and business networking. Founding Diamond Star Networking helped me know I was finally on the right track. It was also very important to me because it became a vehicle through which I could host charity events for homeless children. Being able to do this has been one of the greatest gifts of my life and part of living my dream.

Although I was now once again very successful professionally, my personal life was not exactly what I had hoped. After several unhappy marriages, I still believed that I could find love again and have that relationship I had always dreamed of. For fourteen years I did everything I could think of to find the "perfect" man for me. I attended singles events, had friends fix me up, and joined dating websites. I was dating, but not finding "the one" I knew was meant for me.

I began studying aspects of the "Law of Attraction" and intuitively felt that I could put this philosophy to work for me. In many ways, it was like the daydreaming I had done as a child, but on a much more focused, conscious, and deliberate level. Using this philosophy helped me make major changes in my life. Living by its principles made me feel powerful, that nothing was beyond my reach. I became a leader of a MasterMind group. I feel this is another opportunity to help people reach their full potential and raise the bar on what they can achieve and create in their lives. There is a combination of energy, excitement, and commitment in this mutually-supportive environment where participants challenge each other to create and implement goals, brainstorm with each other, and offer honest support, respect, and compassion.

By applying these principles, I now had a much clearer path and greater tools for finding my perfect mate. I knew I would attract him to me and my life would be complete ... and I did. When we really believe, it is amazing what can happen in our lives.

Always driven to accomplish more and help other people, I co-authored a book, *Blueprint for Success,* in which I outlined my proven and successful strategies for business networking. To be a published author on a topic I am passionate about was another dream come true. At that point, I felt it was time to move to another level. What could be better, more fulfilling, and create more happiness than to help others find their perfect partners? So many people are tired of the usual ways of meeting people and not really making that perfect connection. With all my experience, learning from my many mistakes, and armed with the principles of attracting what you truly want, I created www.sherialmatchmaker.com, where I match people who are seeking their perfect partners. This is most gratifying. I know what it's like to feel lonely and have a strong desire to share life with a partner who makes your heart sing and with whom there is mutual love, trust, and passion.

I have come a long way from an unhappy, abusive, and deprived childhood. I believe that part of my life, as unhappy as it was, has made me a stronger, more compassionate, and self-confident person. I had many obstacles to overcome, both inside myself and because of my life's circumstances. I learned to think outside the box and trust my heart, ability, and intuition. I was a self-made millionaire once and will do it again. I have no doubt about that. I no longer doubt myself. I feel more like a "teenager" now than ever before in my life. I feel young and full of hope with the promise that tomorrow will be even better. I laugh a lot and truly enjoy every aspect of my life. I know that life takes many turns and twists and things don't always turn out the way you want or expect. I also know that I have the internal power and fortitude to deal with anything that comes my way. We attract what we think about. I've learned the great gift of how to change my thoughts to change my life and want to share this knowledge with others on every level.

About the Author

Sherial Bratcher has a passion for bringing people together and is founder and CEO of Diamond Star Networking Events and www.PerfectMatchBySherial.com, both located in Las Vegas. Sherial is a contributing writer to www.vegascommunityonline.org and www.tradeshowlifestyles.com. In 2007 and 2008, she hosted a local radio program. She has represented nationally known speakers and authors from around the world. Equipped with heart, intuition, and business savvy, Sherial is one of Las Vegas' premiere philanthropists, hosting many charity galas. She has owned several businesses, held government contracts in excess of $2 million, and developed supported-employment programs for the disabled.

Sherial utilizes both her personal and professional experience to help people live their dreams in every area of life and make the shift from the ordinary to the extraordinary. She is an innovative businesswoman who brings a fresh, compassionate approach to business and social networking. Sherial believes in "The Law of Attraction" and practices it each and every day. This not only helps her daily life, but also creates an inspirational atmosphere for everyone around her.

Sherial Bratcher can be contacted at:
sherial@sherialbratcher.com
(702) 285-8984

A Better Way to Live

ANDREA CHESTNUT

I don't know how other people live, but it has to be better than this. I must be adopted because people's real parents don't treat their real children this way.

Growing up in the fifties meant everybody knew what was going on, but nobody spoke about it. Being female made me the center of attention for my father. Not in the loving, caring, protective sort of way little girls deserve to experience. My father was the one I needed protection from. When I was nine years old, I got up enough nerve to tell my mother what had been going on.

She said, "I thought something was happening," and even as a nine-year-old, I thought, "Then why didn't you do something to take care of me?"

I was never allowed to have friends over because my father, I now realize as an adult, was a pedophile. So I had no friends come to my house and I couldn't go to theirs because of my mother's fear that their fathers could be the same. My father drank and would become very mean. Beatings were common, followed with touching me and, "you know daddy loves you."

He would also play Russian roulette with me. It went like this: "Stand over there. Now don't move; keep your eyes on me." If I closed my eyes, he would shoot into the ceiling, which made me so scared I would pee on myself. Then would come the laughter, but I learned to be very still. He always carried a gun because of his fear that some jealous husband would come after him. I know for sure I have three half-siblings.

I would hide in the closet and pull my stuffed animals around me thinking if I was not seen, then I'd be safe. Being safe is still an important part of life for me. The police would come to our house about once a month because some concerned neighbor would call. At that time, there weren't any shelters for women. My father had alienated us from any form of family and my mother had no income, no car, and he swore he would kill us kids and make her watch, then kill her if she left. He had stabbed her a couple of times and shot at her more than once. More times than not, he just plain beat her with his fist. He worked the night shift and would come home about one in the morning and the terror would begin. If he was drinking, which was two or three nights a week in addition to the weekends, he would often drag me out of bed to see him. His little girl. Then it would start and if my mother was out of sight, his hands would be in places no father should touch his little girl.

The holidays were always frightening because you never knew what to expect. The year I was eleven, things were really bad. Dad started drinking at Thanksgiving and it continued until January third, when it all came to a stop. My parents had decided to move us, five kids by this time, and themselves into a very small trailer behind the store they had opened. It was a small little grocery store and gas station. They laid every concrete block of the building themselves. It was going to be a new beginning and it was, but not as it was planned.

It can get cold in January in the Atlanta area and this year seemed colder than most. It was in the low thirties that night. My father had been drinking and no one was getting any sleep. The beatings were really bad. We kids were told to go outside because he had to talk to our mother. It was the middle of the night and all we had on were pajamas. Our feet were bare. 'Talk to mother' meant she was going to get hurt. All I could do was try to take care of the younger ones.

My father had heavy duty copper commercial wire that he had used to wire the store. That night he used it to fashion a club. This is what he was using to beat us kids and my mother. It was forty-six years ago and I can still hear my mother pleading for him to stop before he killed one of us. No one escaped his wrath that night, not even my three-year-old sister.

Life Choices: Navigating Difficult Paths

People talk about life-changing events. Well, that night was one of my biggest. By 1:36 a.m. on January 3, 1963, my father was lying in a pool of blood. I can see his foot and hand and his robe, as well as the pool of blood even today.

My father never gave my mother anything for Christmas, but Christmas of 1962 was different. His paranoia was spilling out everywhere. He gave my mother a Brownie Pistol, even though he knew she was afraid of guns. He said she needed it now that they had the store. The night of January 3, she had slipped the gun into the pocket of her housecoat. She later said she knew it all had to stop because he was going to kill one of us. She shot him dead that night.

I saw it all take place and yes, it is true that life goes into slow motion at times like that. My mother called the police and was kept in a cell with the doors open that night. We lived in a very small town and everyone knew what was happening. At the hearing the next day, the judge looked at my mother, called her by name, and said, "I don't know why you didn't do it sooner." The saying that 'life goes on' took on new meaning. Looking back, it was strange how we tried to be normal while not even knowing what normal was. Dysfunction will take its own course unless there is a vision of something different.

Mother contracted cervical cancer when I was sixteen and once again life took a turn. Mom was very sick and had many surgeries over the next three years. We were pretty much left on our own with me trying to be the caretaker for all and not knowing how. Time just went by in a blur of tears and sadness, leaving open holes of dark emptiness.

Mom died the day after Thanksgiving; I was nineteen. I always felt I was on my own, but now it was for sure. I didn't know how other people lived, but it had to be better than this. It is said that as children, by the time we are six years old, we are pretty much set in our patterns of how we approach life. I believe this can be true. I also believe I have choices that as a child I did not have. As an adult, I can make my life different. I had to find a way, a better way, to live.

Even though in the beginning, forgiveness was the last thing I could consider, I slowly realized it was all I could do if I ever expected to be at peace. Forgiveness for me was freeing. It meant I no longer had to keep living my childhood pain over and over. It meant I no longer had to live in shame and loneliness. It set me free to choose a different life. The memories are still clear and pop up at unexpected times. The beauty is those memories are now more like old friends that have given me a life of hope and expectation. I now know life is good and as an adult, how I feel and think about anything is my choice. Just because I forgave my parents did not mean what they did to their children was okay. I came to understand the forgiveness was for me, not them. This understanding has helped me move on in so many areas of life. As long as I was unforgiving, I was a prisoner of my past. Now I smile more easily, I laugh out loud, and life has a texture that I could not touch before. Considering where I came from and the background I had, I could have ended up a prostitute, a drug addict, an alcoholic, in jail, or perhaps even dead. I chose forgiveness and instead, became the successful person I am today.

Looking back over my life, I think of myself as a bumble bee. Bumble bees are not supposed to be able to fly. Their wings are not big enough to lift their bodies. The only reason bumble bees fly is because they don't know they are not supposed to, so they do it anyway.

I chose to be like a Bumble Bee and fly! I chose a better way to live!

About the Author

Andrea Chestnut lives in Las Vegas, Nevada, a world beyond where she began. She owns Chestnut Unlimited, a company specializing in creating environments that inspire people where they live and work. Andrea is surrounded with many friends from all walks of life near and far. Andrea appreciates being able to share her life story, speaking openly to groups and organizations. Her story of inspiration shows life can be more than your history.

Andrea Chestnut can be contacted at:
achestnut@chestnutunlimited.com

Opportunity

There are always two choices. Two paths to take. One is easy. And its only reward is that it's easy.

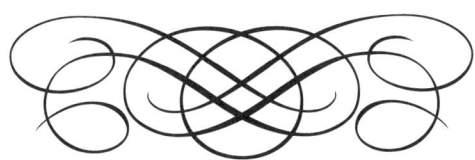

There's a Story for That

DEBORAH D. CLARK

According to Webster's dictionary, a turning point is, "A point in which a decision is made." We make decisions every day; many, many, decisions, over and over again. That's what we do. We make decisions to get up, get dressed, and go out of the house. Where we go and what we do is who we are. When we make a decision, it's a choice. The choices we make determine the lives we live. Very often the choices we make are because of opportunities presented to us. Things come up, things go around, sometimes they pass you. Sometimes they are right in your face and you don't act on them. How can you not do that? It's right there and you have to make a choice. If you don't make a choice, that in itself is a choice and you will have to live with the consequences either way.

My new words of wisdom are, "You have to have a plan." You need to write down what you want to see happen in your life, with your life. I admit that I never had a plan; I just had a dream. I wanted to get married, as do most young girls. But that is another story.

Let me continue. I like to think that mine has been a life of opportunities. I have taken advantage of opportunities that enabled me to have experiences I never would have had otherwise. I have had jobs that allowed me to live in five different states. Not necessarily places I would have moved to on my own, but because I was given the opportunity. I learned something in each place. I experienced things that otherwise I would not have. It enabled me to grow as a person. It made me a stronger person. It opened my mind to possibilities. The world is huge. Never forget that, and remember to make your personal world as big as you can make it. You may think you do not have the means individually, but maybe there are some opportunities around that you are not taking advantage of.

I have also made choices that were very poor decisions. Personal loss and tragedy creates an entirely different set of circumstances, completely changing the picture of your world. My mother's death was such an event. Her death was the most devastating experience of my life. Of all the things I imagined about my life, I never thought she would not be here with me. I made the decision not to keep trying to kill myself after my mother died. I was not trying to slit my wrists, but I was participating in a series of events that had suicidal tendencies. I was developing a pattern of reckless behavior. I was making poor choices. I was so lost, I missed her so much, and I wanted to die. If I had not made the decision to live, I would not be writing this today.

That period in my life is what I call the 'dark times.' I don't remember a lot of what I did. Our minds spare us the reruns. Some things we don't need to see again. There are times in our lives when we hear about what we did, and think to ourselves, "Who was that person?" Those are the dark times. One day I heard my mother say, "Stop." Her voice just popped into my head, and I heard her, so I stopped. She had never really left me, and when she saw that I was not doing well, she put the thought in my head to stop. I said to myself, "No, I am not going to do this anymore." I was blessed to be able to stop. That was a very good choice.

It is important to remember our darkest times. Not all of the incidents per se, but the dark time in general. It is important to know that we can come out of a dark time, and our lives go on. Just like that it stops, they stop, you stop, and you move on. You are more thankful for your life, your family, and your faith. Keep your faith. It's what holds you together; it is what saves you from the dark times.

When you think about the decisions you have made, the choices that make up your life, what do you see? Make it what you want it to be. Start today, right now.

The last relocation was to Maryland. I lived there for several years, but compared to the moves I had made in the past, it was by far the most difficult for me. The move itself was hurried and last minute. I was having trouble finding a job, and a friend suggested I try looking there. When I say difficult, I guess I mean it felt forced. I felt forced to do something, and here was an opportunity. I liked Maryland. I had visited my friend there several times, and thought Maryland was very green compared to my very gray city environment. It seemed okay, so I moved, though I had no plan or job. Again, here was my claim to fame, an opportunity, so I went.

My job there was the hardest-working job I ever had. I had never had a job that required so much 'hustle.' I don't know how else to describe it. I wore many hats and learned so many things. It was very, very busy, all the time. While I was working like crazy, things at the house were much more hectic than I was used to. My roommate was having some issues and the atmosphere was very stressful. I got ill and had to have surgery. It was not fun, not fun at all. Right after that, my roommate unexpectedly moved to Virginia and I had to find another apartment. I was left alone to live in a town where I had no friends or family, just a job. I was exhausted and still working all the time. I had not recuperated properly from my surgery, and the job was taking its toll on my health.

Eventually, I chose to come home. It turned out to be a very good choice because that decision started the life I am living right now. It was the turning point for me. That was the decision that gave me an opportunity to learn how to live with myself. That was the decision that showed me what I can really do. That was the decision that brought me to the place where I got yet another opportunity. When you have been to the dark place, had a bad time in your life, there's a story for that; this is my story.

I believe my life has been a series of opportunities. One of those opportunities was a chance to become a member of Toastmasters International. If you are not familiar, Toastmasters International is an organization that offers a warm and supportive environment for individuals to improve their speaking and leadership skills. I have been a member of Toastmasters for three years. I have held an officer position each one of those three years.

When I joined Toastmasters in October 2006, I had never heard of the organization. I had experience speaking in front of small groups and

There's A Story For That

facilitated training sessions. I really didn't think I needed it. I was not afraid to speak. I was always eager to present to the group. I had been a manager, had trained staff, and had presented to groups on more than one occasion. I saw no reason to join Toastmasters.

I wanted to believe I didn't need it. In reality, quite often I had been told that I talked fast, and people would have a hard time understanding me. Whenever that happened, I would stop and repeat, stop and repeat, but it was always with an almost arrogant air of, "So sorry you didn't get it." I was so wrong, and had been wrong for a long time.

After attending the very first meeting I was amazed to learn what public speaking was all about. I was introduced to the three parts of a speech: opening, body, and closing. I learned the importance of introducing yourself. I understood why you should always explain your objective. It was an eye-opening event. When I had to give my first speech, I was nervous, I still talked a little fast, but I DID IT! You may be surprised to find that when you have specific objectives, the speech is very different.

I became a club officer almost from the start of my membership, becoming the vice president of public relations only three months after I joined. The position became available and I took advantage of the opportunity.

I attended the executive board meetings and presented several ideas to market the club within our company, hosting a newsletter. In 2007, I competed in the speech contest for my club with my tenth speech from the Competent Communicator Manual. This is the first module for the communications track for Toastmasters. I represented my club at the area contest, and came in second. It was a very exciting experience for me. Later that year, I became an area governor. I was responsible for five clubs. It was quite a challenge! I visited other clubs, gave speeches, and encouraged participation. I was outside of the comfort zone of my home club. It was a different world out there!

In 2008, I accepted the division governor position. The same year, I was elected president of my local club. To date I have completed forty speeches. I have continued to train officers, I have been a target speaker for speech competitions, and I have been a speaker at the annual Joint Pharmaceutical Meeting. My proudest accomplishment was presenting a workshop at the first District 83 Fall Conference in November 2008. I now tell everyone to join Toastmasters. Please don't just join, participate. Make the choice to take advantage of every opportunity. There's a story for that—write it.

About the Author

As a niche professional speaker, Deborah Clark knows how to deliver programs that provide value to audiences. With a background in all aspects of meeting development, staff training, and event organization, she understands how to meet her clients' needs for a successful event. Her client list includes adult school/continuing education programs, professional associations, non-profit groups, and private clients. In addition to being a professional speaker, Deborah is an active community volunteer through Jersey Cares.

Deborah Clark can be contacted at:
Dclark6581@gmail.com
www.dclark6581.com
Phone: (877) 827-7003
Fax: (862) 902-1579

When Opportunity Knocks

EDIE RAETHER

When opportunity knocks, do you open the door—or complain about the noise? Opportunity is often a matter of perception. Within our vision of the world is the image of ourselves. It may seem like some people have all the luck; they are randomly chosen. Yet, often luck is not random at all, but a time when preparation and opportunity come together.

Although opportunity is often a result of what we create, we must first recognize it to tap into it. To recognize opportunity, you must be a possibility thinker and also have the ability to predict patterns and trends. For example, at a time when most people are losing their life's savings in the stock market, my son's guidance gave me returns that no stock broker has ever accomplished for me. It is simply his ability to predict trends, observe patterns, and change his thinking as the economy shifts from a bull to a bear market. Crisis is opportunity in disguise, but only for those who define it as such.

George Soros, a hedge fund manager, whose team of analysts made him millions during the bear market of the '70s, fired his staff in the early '80s when he predicted a bull market. The reason was because he feared they would not change their thinking. The decisions that create wealth in a bear market are not the same strategies required for success in a bull market. In a bull market, when stocks fall one buys with the assumption they will go up. In a bear market, one must resist the temptation and break free of conditioned responses and behavior that was previously rewarded.

Recognizing opportunity is dependent upon your ability to scan the environment, for opportunities are everywhere, but we need to recognize them, see the potential, create a strategy, an action plan, and then muster the courage to take the risks necessary to move forward. However, it may not be as much a factor of what you do, but what you must not do.

One of the reasons people don't see opportunity when it is painted on a billboard and screaming louder than thunder is because of limited thinking and cerebral myopia. Oftentimes, it may be due to negativity, but it may also be due to simply not being visionary and seeing the big picture. Unfortunately, creativity is often stifled by our education system. Corporations tend to be risk-adverse, and yet calculated risk-taking is essential for opportunities created by innovation. In other words, when you find yourself in deep water, become a diver!

Learning to dive has become crucial to my survival. While left-brain people are often too cautious and are snagged by analysis paralysis, right-brain people can tend to dive into deep water before learning how to swim. Being an off-the-chart right-brain optimist, everything appears to be an opportunity when, in fact, it may be a serious derailment. I bought a dozen pay phones, although given fair warning not to do so. From the crooks who sold them to me, referred to as the Cuban Mafia, to the installer who collected his fees but never did the job, it was proposed residual income that had a tainted residue.

When I moved to North Carolina in 1997, being a realtor seemed to require simply taking orders, so, of course, I became a licensed realtor. There have also been dozens of MLMs or multi-level marketing opportunities. While the concept is great, and many of the products were useful, once again it was another distraction from my doing what was meaningful and purposeful for me.

A former husband's embezzlement was also disguised as opportunity, as was a stock broker who, because I took action, is now selling ice cream instead. No, it's not your neighborhood Dilly Bar Man! Then there were the real estate opportunities that got washed away by Hurricane Fran. They were sold to me by a realtor who had previously been imprisoned on felony charges. Nothing is ever a good deal when you deal with bad people. More recently I loaned money to a private investor because he guaranteed very competitive interest rates and even backed up the loan with real estate that, wouldn't you know, went into foreclosure. The point I am making is that promises are not opportunities.

Because of my random lust for opportunity, I squandered not only years of my life, but also my life's savings chasing the next promised opportunity. I lost millions of hard-earned dollars. No sugar daddies and no winning the lottery! The more I lost, the more fear and desperation sought opportunity that was promised by every slick salesperson I encountered. If it sounds too good to be true, it probably is, but not when it is music that makes you want to dance.

Upon moving to North Carolina and leaving behind a very lucrative psychotherapy practice, I had built a lovely home which is referred to as Edie's Mansion on the Home and Garden channel (HGTV). It must be their big hit as they have been showing it for years! It is still not sold. Although I could be living in the mansion, since I am paying the mortgage and the renter tends to forget to put the check in the mail, I am often sleeping on my modest nineteen-foot boat while renting out my cottage on lovely Lake Norman. It helps pay the four mortgages on properties that total over two million. Heck, Suzy Orman slept in her car shortly before her breakthrough, so it is probably a good omen.

As defined by my son Tory, opportunity is the chance to make progress toward a stated goal. That was the problem. I either had too many goals or I was not clear on which ones were authentic. Are your goals allowing you to be true to yourself?

Possibilities are only opportunities if they push you gently down the path toward your committed goals and desires. You must sort out and be selective. If you can't say "no" to possibilities that are not in sync with your instincts, your core genius or soul's code, you are simply out of focus. You either get busy living, or you get busy dying. Some degree of skepticism can be a virtue if it brings balance to your decision making. Ask yourself:

What gives my life meaning?
What makes me happy?
How do I choose to serve and make a difference?

I probably should have read some of my own books. In *Why Cats Don't Bark (Unleash Your PowerZone, Intuitive Intelligence: The Other IQ)*,

I encourage people to trust their gut guidance to discover and manifest their core genius which is revealed between the ages of about three to seven. As a result of that book and another I had written, *Winning! How Winners Think – What Champions Do*, I discovered that all champions interviewed had a flash of their greatness at a young age. The reason Oprah Winfrey, Tiger Woods, Jack Canfield, Barbra Streisand, Michael Jordan, and many others had achieved exceptional success was because they not only recognized opportunity but were determined to make a difference.

Sometimes opportunity whispers softly in our ear, but we have to listen. Other times it's a loud crash such as a disastrous, life-changing event, and we have to take action. Again, my question is, when opportunity knocks, do you open the door or complain about the noise? Do you recognize it? Do you take action and create it? Opportunity is not a passive, but an action verb that only you can exercise. Waiting for opportunity is like waiting for the sun to shine on a cloudy day.

Tired of waiting for the market to kick into high gear, I realized that I had to create my own opportunities independent of outside circumstances or the economic environment. I learned that opportunity is about choice. It is making a decision to bash on regardless!

Being inspired by two of my books and my grandchildren, I had an idea of how I could change the way the world thinks, one mind at a time. In the midst of total chaos and financial challenges, *I Believe I Can Fly*, the first in a series of children's character-building programs, took flight in the fall of 2009. At the same time I released a book, *What Most Builders Won't Tell Women (or Men) - 101 Ways to Save Big Bucks on Your Next House*. I had built several homes and had both good and bad builders. The last builder went bankrupt for the second time and had used my "draws" to cover the expenses for his spec houses. He dragged out the building of my personal residence over a period of nearly three years. I spent years and thousands more correcting his mistakes and negligence.

A couple of years ago the "aha" moment came when I realized I could recover my losses. By writing a book on building tips, I could help others learn from my mistakes. Now, we don't have a contract yet, but we do intend to get an order from Home Depot and Lowes for a million books. Now, that would certainly offset my losses!

Opportunities stop only when we stop thinking ... BIG. Since I also encountered serious losses from a stock broker, I am now working on another book, "What Most Financial Advisors Won't Tell Women (or Men)." Again, the intention is not to put a bad mark on any profession but to prevent consumers from being snagged by those who don't belong in any respectable profession in the first place. The momentum continues with a complete series including, "What Most Lawyers Won't Tell Women (or Men)," "What Most Doctors Won't Tell Women (or Men)," and so forth.

The point I am making is that we create our own opportunities with a positive mind state and belief system sustained by an undying determination and desire to dodge defeat. The choice is yours. Choice is a freedom that only you can relinquish, if you choose to do so. As J.L. Moreno, the father of psychodrama once proclaimed, "The greatest power in our being is that we choose our thoughts. I choose, therefore I am free."

Frequently people have messed up potential opportunities because of not understanding how good decisions are made. For example, life coaches often recommend that you follow your bliss or find your passion. "Do what you love doing and the money will follow" has long been the mantra of many. However, the money may not follow when a logical procedure is not followed.

Capitalizing on opportunity requires a strategic plan and also the ability to execute positive action at the right time. The Path to Self-Discovery, developed by T. Falcon Napier, is a color-coded model that provides a sequence in making decisions that prevents regrets and assures results.

    White (Snow) — Get the hard, cold facts.
    Green(Grass) — Set goals for growth.
    Black (Night) — Identify obstacles.
    Yellow (Sun) — Solutions to the problem.
    Red (Fire) — Connect with your passion and intuition to know how your choices feel.
    Blue (Sky) — The CEO or overall seer of the process to making good decisions.

When Opportunity Knocks

So many good ideas and opportunities are lost or not sustained because of not following this sequence. When you leap, the net may not always be there. Once you identify your passion, due diligence is essential to get the hard, cold facts. Although you may be clear on your goals, without knowing the obstacles and possible problems, you could waste your life's savings on a dream—that ends up as a nightmare. By identifying and then removing the obstacles, solutions are clear and thus your problems can be solved. Before moving forward, do a gut check on how your decision checks out with your heart. In other words, if it comes from your head, check it out with your heart before you take action, and if it comes from your heart, run it through your head for an objective check and balance to emotional choices. Following this sequence when making decisions will transform possibilities into true opportunities that promise to increase your ROI—Return On Intelligence, and also your joy.

About the Author

Edie Raether, MS, CSP, is an international speaker, trainer, and best-selling author who promises to challenge the way you think, and change the way you do business. Her six books have been translated into numerous languages and include: *Why Cats Don't Bark, Winning!, Sex for the Soul, Forget Selling, What Most Builders Won't Tell Women (or Men),* and *I Believe I Can Fly* (a character-building program for children). She has also co-authored ten anthologies, and is an expert resource for hundreds of publications such as *The Wall Street Journal, USA Today,* the *New York Times, INC,* and Reuters.

With thirty-five years of coaching experience in behavioral psychology and change, Edie has also been a college professor and talk show host with ABC. She is a certified speaking professional. The CSP is the highest earned designation awarded by the National Speakers Association to fewer than 8 percent of its membership worldwide.

Edie Raether can be contacted at:
edie@raether.com
www.raether.com
(704) 658- 8997

The Choice That Changed My Life Forever

JUDI MOREO

A gorgeous 6' 2", blond-haired, brown-eyed photographer was actually standing in the doorway to my office, laughing and smiling, saying, "Come with me to South Africa."

I had never been outside of America. And I had a modeling agency to run. I hadn't taken off for a holiday in six years. His invitation was tempting, but I didn't feel I could take the time for a vacation or holiday. So I thanked him and shrugged it off. Perhaps one day I'd have time for holidays.

My secretary came into my office and asked, "Did *he* just invite you to go with *him* to South Africa, visit his home country and meet his parents?"

"Yes," I said. "Wouldn't he be surprised if I actually went?" Then, the idea struck me. "Buy me a ticket," I told my secretary, "And get me the seat next to his. It will be a wonderful joke. After we show him the ticket and see what he says, we'll cash it back in."

She bought the ticket. The next time he came into my office, I showed it to him and, sure enough, he was surprised.

"I invite everyone to come to South Africa," he said, "but no one ever accepts. I will call my mother and have her make arrangements for you." Out he went.

What great fun! We had called his bluff and were thoroughly enjoying our little joke. About an hour later, my secretary came in and said, "I think the joke is on us. I didn't realize I bought you a non-refundable ticket."

Life Choices: Navigating Difficult Paths

What started out as nothing more than a joke ended up becoming the choice that changed my life forever.

I met my photographer friend, Vimmi, at the airport and within an hour, we were on our way to South Africa. I couldn't recall ever having been so excited. I must have asked him one hundred questions in the first hour on the plane. He explained to me in no uncertain terms that he was going home to see his family and had no intention of entertaining a foreigner by doing touristy things and sightseeing. Once we changed planes in New York, he took a sleeping pill and went to sleep, leaving me to my excitement and questions. I read the literature that my secretary had collected for me. I learned about Johannesburg, Pretoria (the capital of South Africa), Durban, Cape Town, and Sun City (a gaming resort in what is called "a homeland"). I watched movies and talked to the people who were seated around me. It was a ten-hour flight from New York to Johannesburg, so there was plenty of time to meet the other passengers and get to know them. Many of them were from South Africa and others had visited before, so they gave me pointers and sightseeing tips.

Vimmi's mother, Marty, met us at the airport in Johannesburg and they drove me to the Landrost Hotel, downtown, where she had made a reservation for me. It was a beautiful, old, historical hotel with dark wood paneling, high ceilings, plush furnishings and Persian rugs. I felt like royalty. Once I was checked in, they left and I went to my room. I was alone. Not only was I alone, I was alone in a foreign country about which I knew nothing except what I had read in those brochures and learned from the people I had talked to on the plane. What was I to do? I had a choice to make. I could stay in my room, hide out, and be safe. Or I could muster up my courage, go out in the streets, see this new country and have an adventure.

Early the next morning, I went down to the lobby and consulted the concierge who told me a tour that day was not possible as I had to make a reservation the previous day. He said he would arrange tours for me for the next three days. Today, he recommended, I should put my money in my boot and my camera in a paper bag and take a walk around downtown. The idea of the paper bag was not to look like a tourist. It wasn't long until I figured out that my disguise probably wasn't working, as my flaming red hair and brightly-colored attire were really out of place in the business district of Johannesburg. Everyone I passed wore grey, black, or tweed business suits. I noticed one man in particular as he was dressed in black and white; everything was stark, beautiful, tailored, and expensive. He was more striking than Tom Selleck at his peak of popularity. This man smiled as he passed me. I was lingering and looking in store windows, noticing the architecture, going in and out of stores, looking at tourist treasures and didn't think too much about it when I passed him again a while later. Once again, he smiled and nodded.

As I stopped for the light before crossing the street at the corner of Coetze and Kline, I happened to look up and see a small outdoor café on the second floor of a building across the street. The cafe was located on an outdoor terrace with many colored umbrellas shading the tables from the sun. I was thinking how beautiful it was when the Tom Selleck look-alike walked up behind me and said something that I didn't understand. So I said to him, "I'm sorry. I only speak English."

"I was speaking English," he replied in a heavy accent.

"What did you say?"

"I said that I've been running up and down this street for a half hour now trying to find out if anyone knew you so they could introduce me, but no one did, so I figured I'd better introduce myself before you get away. I'm Jeff Hoffman."

"Well, nice to meet you, Mr. Hoffman."

"Would you like to have a coffee?" he asked, indicating we should go to that charming café that I had been admiring. I saw no harm in sitting in an outdoor café, having coffee with the most handsome man I had seen in many years, so I agreed to go for "a coffee."

Mr. Hoffman turned out to be divorced, a few years older than me, a successful businessman, and very interesting. He offered to show me around Johannesburg, but I explained that I had tours booked for the next few days. He then suggested that he drive me back to my hotel. I said that if he'd like to walk me back and point out the sites of downtown, I would be happy to have him accompany me. So we walked, talked, and arrived at the hotel a couple of hours later. He invited me to dinner and I agreed, as long as it was in the dining room at the hotel. After all, I was in a foreign country and didn't know him at all. After dinner, he said "good night" and that he would call.

The next day, I took my first tour. I had fun talking to people whom I probably never would have talked with had I not been alone. I met people from England, Australia, and Asia. We saw the city, watched a performance of African dancers, toured a gold mine, and even panned for gold. As the bus pulled up to let me off at my hotel, I saw Jeff Hoffman standing on the curb.

"Hi," I said. "What are you doing here?"

"I've come to make sure you get a good dinner," he said. Once again, we had a fabulous meal and enjoyed talking with each other about our different cultures and our lives. I was fascinated with his life and he was happy to share his experiences with me.

Each evening, as I returned from my daily tour, Jeff was standing at the bus stop waiting to take me to dinner. Then I went on a three-day tour to the Kruger National Park, where I photographed animals in the wild. Everyone on the tour slept in round huts with thatched roofs called rondovals. In the Kruger Park, all eight of us who were on the tour ate our meals together and had cocktails called "sundowners" in the bush as we watched the sun go down. We even had dinner in the bush ... a fabulous dinner served on folding tables with white tablecloths, china, and even candles. Later we observed the night creatures as they came out of their daily hiding. What a wonderful adventure I was having.

Sure enough, when the tour bus pulled up to return me to the Landrost, Jeff was there again. He said that by now he figured I would need some clean clothes. He had come to take me to dinner and pick up my dirty laundry. He said that I should not pay the high hotel prices for having my laundry done, but give it to him and he would ask his maid to do it for me which he did. Then, when we were together again on Friday evening, he suggested that on Saturday he would take me to the Indian market. Surely, I could trust him enough by now to get in his car. After all, he had returned my clothing!

So Saturday I made the choice to go with him to the Indian market, where we shopped, ate exotic Indian foods, laughed, walked, and shopped some more. He invited me to his home for dinner.

On Sunday morning, Vimmi called wondering where I had been. They hadn't heard from me all week and were beginning to worry. He said he was also feeling guilty that he had dropped me downtown and left me on my own to fend for myself. I told him I was having a wonderful time, but he insisted that I go with him and his mother to Sun City, the gambling mecca in Bophutaswana, to see an entertainer by the name of Julio Iglesias. Julio was not yet known in the United States, so I had never heard of him, but I felt it would be fun to travel and see a bit more of the country. I packed up my bags and went off with Vim and Marty to see Julio's show.

Marty had forgotten to fill up the gas tank in the car which caused us to run out of gas halfway to our destination. So I called Jeff and he brought us some "petrol" for the car. Marty invited him to join us on our trip, but he said he didn't want to impose; after all, he had a business to run.

We were late arriving in Sun City and had missed most of the show. We made our way into the showroom in our traveling clothes, just in time to see Julio sing his last song. Marty was very upset. The tickets had cost her a lot of money and she had really wanted to see Julio's show. Not knowing who he was, but being from Las Vegas, I said I was sure that we'd be able to go backstage and meet him. So we marched up to Stage Door 4 where a group of ladies were screaming and jumping up and down. I walked right to the front of the crowd with Marty in tow, presented my Las Vegas modeling agency business card to the security guard, and said, "Please tell Julio that I'm here." Before long the security guard came back with a gentleman who asked us to follow him.

Back stage, reporters from around the world waited to interview Julio, as waiters in black tails and white gloves served champagne and hors d'oeuvres. Needless to say, we were a bit underdressed in our traveling jeans and t-shirts. I even had a chocolate drip on the front on my shirt—the result of having eaten a candy bar in the car after it had melted in the sun. Julio entered the room with my card in his hand and said, "Judi, how nice of you to come."

"This is my friend, Marty," I said. "She so wanted to see your show but we ran out of gasoline and were late and missed all but the last song. Please, will you autograph her program?"

He not only autographed the program, he took Marty's face in his hands, kissed her on the cheeks, and sang her a song. She was blown away! He then greeted the press, thanked everyone for coming and when we finished our drinks, we said our goodbyes. Marty and I were like teenage girls as we went outside and sat on the patio, giggling, not believing that we had managed to get in backstage and that Julio actually sang to her and kissed her cheeks. She swore she would never wash her face again.

The following morning, we went out to sit by the pool and Julio was already there. He called to us, "Judi … Marty … come and say hello." We were ecstatic. We spent the day swimming, parasailing, and waterskiing. We ran into some friends from Las Vegas who now danced in the production show at the Sun City Hotel. It was such a glorious day; it was incredibly beautiful there and we had such a wonderful time.

When I got back to my room, there was a message to call Jeff, so I did. He asked if he could take me out to a small town about fifty kilometers outside of the city to meet his father, sister, and her family when I returned to Johannesburg.

That, too, turned out to be a wonderful outing. His family members were all so nice and asked many questions about America and my life there. They served a wonderful meal and told me about their lives.

Vimmi then decided I should go to Cape Town to the beach for a few days with Marty and him. It was the most beautiful place I had ever seen. Vim and I laid on the beach in the sun and watched gorgeous people walk by; everyone was friendly and they all smiled at us. I was sure they were smiling because they somehow knew I was from America. Vimmi swore they were smiling at him. We enjoyed granadilla popsicles at the beach, ate out at the Greek restaurant on the corner down from Marty's apartment, and drove around the Cape, giving real baboons rides on the hood of the car around the downtown area. I was fascinated by how the baboons would wait on the side of the road for cars going out to the beach, jump on the car and ride one way; later, they'd jump on a car to ride back to the edge of the city. Imagine … hitchhiking baboons!

Jeff called every night and when we arrived back in Johannesburg once again, he was waiting for me. I only had two days left before I was to return home. We spent almost every waking second together … sightseeing, shopping; we even attended his son's cricket game.

When the day came for me to return home, Jeff drove me to the airport to say goodbye. We stopped at a restaurant near the airport to have lunch. As we finished lunch, this wonderful, stylish, kind man with dark hair and dark eyes pulled out a small box and gave it to me. I opened it and discovered a beautiful, handmade gold ring set with a champagne diamond. Jeff smiled at me and said, "Come back to South Africa and be my wife."

I definitely had a choice to make. It took me two years before I made the decision to say yes. I closed up my home in Las Vegas and made all the arrangements to move to South Africa. Shortly before we were to be married, Jeff's brother-in-law called and told me that Jeff had died.

Needless to say, I had another choice to make. I made the choice to move to South Africa anyway, which was the beginning of the adventure of my life. I lived in South Africa eight years before I returned home. It was the best decision I ever made. Living in another country, especially that country throughout the end of apartheid, changed my life forever.

About the Author

Judi Moreo is the author of *You Are More Than Enough: Every Woman's Guide to Purpose, Passion, and Power*, and it's companion, *Achievement Journal*. She is an award-winning businesswoman and motivational speaker. Her superb talent for customizing programs to meet organizational needs has gained her a prestigious following around the world. Her passion for living an extraordinary life is mirrored in her zeal for helping others realize their potential and achieve their goals. With her dynamic personality and style, she is an unforgettable speaker, inspiring motivator, and an exceptional life coach.

Judi Moreo may be contacted at:
judi@judimoreo.com
www.judimoreo.com
www.youaremorethanenough.com
Turning Point International
P. O. Box 231360, Las Vegas, Nevada 89105
(702) 896-2228

Independence

Your life is the sum result of all the choices you make, both consciously and unconsciously. If you can control the process of choosing, you can take control of all aspects of your life. You can find the freedom that comes from being in charge of yourself.

—*Joanne Kathleen Rowling*

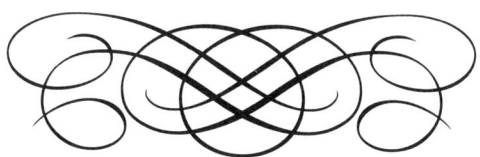

Defining Moment: You Are Fired!

JESSE FERRELL

You are fired! Yes, you ... your services are no longer wanted here.

If you have never been fired, you are missing out on one of life's universal defining moments that has the potential to set great transformation and growth into motion. It can also be a devastating blow that serves up the dreaded crippling sucker-punch from your blind spot. Your attitude and how you respond to this defining moment will determine which paradigm becomes your reality.

I have heard it said that in many industries you are only as good as your last day of work. Well, that tired axiom can be much closer in terms of reality for some of us. Here's a new adage for you—try this on—you are only as good as your last decision. How does that leave you feeling? Could this enlist feelings of unworthiness, anxiety, plummeted self-esteem, shame, resentment, anger, despair, and fear? These are surely universal emotions. They stir the pot of internal strife when you discover that your last decision is all that your employer believes you are worth, just before he lowers the boom and fires you. Can you relate to this situation?

I can. Eight years ago I was enjoying a steady rise to the top of casino marketing royalty in Las Vegas, Nevada, working for what most view as the number one hotel and casino in the industry. Customers and industry buffs alike knew that once you landed a position at this premier property, you were considered to have elevated your game to playing with the best that the hospitality industry has to offer. It felt great! I had arrived, or so I thought.

Defining Moment: you Are Fired!

After years of giving the resort my very best customer service skills, education, and sharply-honed people-caring skills, I received a call at 5:00 p.m. from my boss's secretary, who asked me to come to my vice president of casino marketing's office right away. I politely responded with, "I'm in the middle of serving a client; I will come down as soon as I finish."

She responded with a sharp and resounding, "NO! You come right now." My customer didn't take kindly to this call to action, abruptly ending the service cycle, rendering it incomplete. I experienced a new level of learning that showed up as a lack of appreciation for a true professional practicing the craft of customer care, customer service, and marketing. It was clear that none of that mattered; in their eyes, my professionalism and value as an executive wasn't good enough to be allowed the common decency of completing my last decision or action for the company.

Please keep in mind that I was a highly-paid executive earning a six-figure annual salary, which left a mark beyond the stinging sensation of being terminated. I found myself wondering if I had gone from the hero making six figures in the morning to the zero making no figures in the evening. Could I have truly been so bad that this was a justifiable fate for such a polished executive? The answer is no. I had not lowered my standard to deserve such a dismissal. I was a victim of circumstances and having highly sophisticated communication and customer service skills was the blade that cut on the wrong side. Those polished skills were the very culprit for my termination.

I recall speaking to a million-dollar casino marketing client about my termination shortly after my departure. Well, I shouldn't really call it speaking; it was more like belly-aching and complaining. Sometime within the first thirty seconds of launching into my highly spirited gripe session, this sophisticated wealthy client stopped me. I will never forget his response; it was truly the crowning jewel in this life-sized defining moment!

He said, "Jess, let me stop you right here. My company is a buy-out, takeover merger specialist. When we come into an organization and run into an employee or executive like you, we just fire them on the spot! And here is your story: **incompetence always drives competence out**!"

Wow! His words penetrated my chest like bullets and permeated my entire being.

I had not even gotten to the part of my diatribe where I explained that all the other executives at my level didn't seem to care for my working style and professionalism. I had not told him about the time when another casino credit line client pulled me outside of the marketing and credit office and said, "You don't have any friends in that room. The entire time that you were setting up my casino credit line, the other executives were making faces and ridiculing you behind your back."

Wow! How did the million-dollar customer know all this without me having to tell him? The answer is found in corporate culture and steadiness of foot. It is found in strength of character and purposeful professionalism; it is discovered in poise and charisma. It shows up in those who have vast pleasing character range coupled with a pleasing personality. All of this can be blinding, intimidating, or leaving the door wide open for resentful, jealous, insecure, and envious types. Think about how clear this picture becomes when you apply the axiom of the millionaire—**"incompetence drives competence out."** I had to be driven out, because although I endeavored to serve internal and external customers with the best of service in mind, that was the very thing that turned many of the other executives against me, the 'I care' part of service. The 'How You Leave Them Feeling' (explore more on this subject in the book entitled *How You Leave Them Feeling* by Jesse Ferrell) aspect of demonstrating your care and service to others through your actions.

This was truly a defining moment for me; I had never been fired or asked to leave any group that I chose to be a part of. This was a first and the sting of this termination lasted for nearly eighteen months.

From this vantage point, I can say that it is the worst and best thing to ever happen to me personally or professionally!

Sitting in the office of the vice-president of casino marketing, I felt a major epiphany emerging. I recall my thoughts with lucid vision. This truly defined the moment. I clearly heard a switch in my head flip like the sound that is made when a circuit breaker is replaced and all the lights of a previously blackened house come back on at once. I said to myself, *never again*! I made a choice that would change my life forever. *Never again*! *Never again* will one man decide my financial fate in an instant, *never again* will one man or one woman, or a group of men or women take my financial and emotional bank account from hero to zero in an instant.

I had a new-found respect for the term 'defining moment' and I vowed to use this moment as a path to greatness, as a way to discover my calling. I knew this was happening just as it should and that it would provide the incentive for me to develop my vocation while living and serving on an entirely different level.

I knew at that moment that it was time for me to exit the rat race and discover my true calling. Also, I knew I had to connect with my best gifts. In order to reverse the cycle of control from others determining my fate to me being in control of my destiny, I had to connect with my major definite purpose. I knew that in the moment my boss said that he felt bad he had to terminate me. In fact, he said, "I stayed up for three nights thinking about having to terminate you."

My response was, "Really?" Then I looked him square in the eyes and said, "Well, if you stayed up for three nights thinking about having to terminate me, how many nights do you think I will stay up having been terminated?" No response to that point. I decided that I was going to maintain my dignity, since ultimately, that was all I had left.

Typically, it is customary for an executive at my level in the operation to be escorted off the property by security immediately following termination. I knew this very well. I had held a number of executive director of marketing positions for most of my sixteen-year casino marketing career, and I had been compelled to use the assistance of security at senior management's insistence upon terminating marketing executives over the years.

Something inside me respected the switch that flipped in my brain and rose up to refuse to allow the above-mentioned humiliation ceremony to become part of my present. On a deeper level, I could feel the winds of honor and integrity grip my soul. I surrendered to the higher power that was resonating within me and discovered the ease of self-trust, coupled with self-respect and the power of intention. This higher power raised my social, environmental, and emotional consciousness and I spoke with eloquence, poise, passion, and purpose.

With purpose leading the way, I said to my vice president, "You have been given the power to fire me, but I possess the personal power and intention to tell you how it is going to be done." My conviction steadied my adamant oration that I refused to be escorted off the property as I had done nothing wrong. I shared my passion for delivering positive and infectious customer service with the power of presence at a sophisticated executive level in and outside of the corporate boardroom.

I reiterated that my value and delivery were unmatched and I refused to be apologetic for providing this exclusive property with anything short of excellence. I added that if my personal and professional signature of striving for excellence was worthy of being considered a terminal offense, then, in fact, he was right, it was time for me to go.

At this juncture, are you wondering what derelict atrocities I had committed in order to have earned the right to be dismissed from an executive position that I had been preparing my entire life to serve? Well here it is, directly from the creative mind of my vice president of marketing. He said, "We are terminating you because you have time management issues and you don't get along with the other guys on the team."

I took a moment to 'stand down' before returning a response. This accusation was so offensive and far out in left field; it couldn't have been further from the truth or further away from reality. The two sharpest pencils in my bag are time management and understanding how to value and get along with others.

During this period I felt my time management was very good, as I designed and maintained an advanced task management system in order to accomplish all that was on my plate. I have heard it said that "if you really want to get something done, you should give it to a busy person." While I remained very busy, I was called upon often to solve minor to major problems in all facets of the organization. I also worked as a substitute teacher for grades kindergarten through high school (up to and including the twelfth grade) and taught a senior level casino marketing class at the University of Nevada at Las Vegas, while handily holding

Defining Moment: you Are Fired!

down a full time job as marketing executive at a major casino resort in Las Vegas. Does this sound like a person with time management issues?

This creative story was the best that my boss could conjure up and I can assure you it was both humiliating and infuriating to hear such unfair and untrue accusations. It really doesn't matter what reason he cited for my termination; it was something that had to happen in order to take me to the next level. I had to either be fed up enough to quit, or someone had to terminate me in order to create the incentive for me to leave the industry and tap into my best skills, strengths, gifts, and talents to serve a greater vision.

I remain thankful and appreciative for having been terminated as I believe my beautiful life now wouldn't exist otherwise. This new-found freedom to choose the route of endless possibilities is enlightening. This exercise in real-life drama and educational moment has been the light of my life and it was ignited in order to lead to my ultimate connection… a connection to my major definite purpose and the development of a global playing field that is best suited for my full compliment of talents. I truly believe that "the educational paradox is a mirror of life and the irony is found in the never ending challenge between providing the best tools and support with the most affordable means of getting there."*

If you choose to face life head-on and refuse to allow challenges or setbacks to set the course for your life, you, too, can move through the stages of disbelief, discovery into a full transformation. If you refuse to simply settle for what life brings you, you will find a world that you don't currently know reshaping your existence. As you continue to read this chapter, ask yourself what's holding you back from pursuing a great life. What will it take for you to release your fears and own your greatness? Will you stop dragging your past into your future, only to fill up your real future with nothing short of continuously repeating the past. How does that thought leave you feeling? The real truth here is what you elect to do about it should you find yourself feeling drained by the reality of continually dragging your past into your future, leaving no opening for possibilities and opportunity to live your most unencumbered and enlightened best life now. To be unencumbered and enlightened with clear purpose, passion and intention, now that is transformation in high gear! One major obstacle that blocks the path of transformation is fear.

In my personal and professional coaching business, I'm constantly being charged with helping clients who feel lost and in need of being released from an ever-present haunting past, the bondage of fear, guilt, shame, paralysis, and apathy. The need to get unstuck and get out of their own way is paramount to their success in order to lay rise to living a full and invigorating life which allows transformation.

The majority of clients I serve who are challenged with moving on from stuck situations are carrying some sort of negative perception from their past into their future. Many of them fill up the circle of their future with their baggage from the past, leaving no room for the future to be any different; like a ball and chain they drag around the stale garbage of the past and infuse their perception of the future with it. As I walk clients through this amazing discovery and recovery process, they are transformed into the blissful place we call 'being present.' This place is where your best life is lived! This is a place where your energies resonate at a higher level with an endless flow of replenishment.

My defining moment of being terminated set in motion my extreme indoctrination into the self-help world and cast me in the role of **'difference maker!'** It is this role that allows me to help others make life transformations. We embark upon the challenging journey of determining what the clients want (wants analysis) and what matters most to them. We build a 'JessTalk What Matters Most' Portfolio and transfer that knowledge into a full-fledged JessTalk Lifestyle Portfolio. This life planning and transformation becomes their roadmap to success in life and shines brightly as a defining moment for them. What choice will you make to awaken that defining moment in your life?

* Quote was developed by Jesse Ferrell and Beth Martinez

About the Author

Jesse Ferrell coaches and energizes professionals, corporate executives, and senior executives on how to get organized, stop procrastinating, and take charge of their personal and professional endeavors. He has amassed more than 54, 540 hours sharing his domestic and international professional speaking, executive corporate training, life coaching, and development programs.

Jesse attended the University of Nevada at Las Vegas on multiple academic scholarships, where he earned a Bachelor of Fine Arts Degree and a second Bachelor of Science degree in Hotel Administration. He worked in the hospitality industry for thirty years and spent six years as an adjunct professor at the University of Nevada at Las Vegas.

Jesse is a recognized published author of multiple articles and books and his personal mission is to make a difference in the world by helping others transform their lives via his national and international coaching programs and speaking platforms. His company makes healthy contributions to foundations in the Dominican Republic and Louis Gossett, Jr.'s ERACISM foundation. His unique life purpose is to champion powerful communication in order to embrace his chosen responsibility of leadership in the role of **'difference maker,'** where the magic of transformational growth is shared!

Jesse Ferrell can be contacted at:
JessTalk Speaking & Coaching Firm
speak@jesstalk.com
www.jesstalk.com
(702) 541-6992 (Office)

Life Choices: Navigating Difficult Paths

Martha, George, and I

DAN ROBERTS

What do TV/celebrity hostess Martha Stewart, New York Yankees owner George Steinbrenner and yours truly have in common? We're all convicted felons.

Ex-con is the common term, but whatever you call it, we are all branded with this scarlet letter for the rest of our lives.

Unlike Martha and George, I was not a multi-millionaire when the "stuff hit the fan." They have no idea what it is like to lose everything in the blink of an eye. My job, my life-long profession, my home, my cars, and bank accounts—everything I had accumulated over my life—gone.

They say every convict has a story. This is mine.

Ask anyone who knows me (and I'll be the first to admit) that I'm not the smartest person in a room. While my college buddies were out partying and enjoying the benefits of youth, I studied. Friday nights for me—as well as the rest of the week—meant going to the library and studying.

Somehow I made it through law school, but failed the New York State Bar—like I said, not the smartest guy in the world—and then made it on the second try and was admitted to the Bar.

Through fate, luck, and more hours working than you can imagine, I became the "man" for the medical transportation industry in New York state. Medical transportation is just a fancy legal term for the private ambulance and wheelchair accessible van companies.

In New York City alone, there were over 150 separate companies—and I knew them all, or more importantly, they knew me as the lawyer to call whenever they had a legal problem. To an attorney's delight, the medical transportation industry was heavily regulated by separate city, state, and federal rules, regulations, and laws. I became the expert on all medical transportation legal issues.

Besides individual company problems that might require my legal services, there were many times when certain governmental agencies would target the industry. Whenever that occurred, I would receive the first frantic phone call, quickly followed by the second, third, fourth, and on and on.

It was not really a question of whether or not I was a great attorney, but mostly the quality of my opposition. It was always a good talking point to remind my clients that the administrative agencies that were challenging them on any given moment were as arrogant as they were incompetent. My win/loss record was quite impressive and my ambulance clients respected me. The administrative agencies did not.

In 1994, after sixteen years of such legal services, circumstances arose where I could practice what I preached to my clients. With members of my family, I was able to purchase a struggling ambulance company.

Life was good. In all candor, it was very good. Interestingly, since ambulances are a 24-hour, 7-day a week, 365 day operation, I was never "off-duty," but while there were killer hours, I never considered it work. The family joke was that a truly successful attorney is one who owns his own ambulance company—and to a certain degree it was true. I became my own "ambulance chaser."

The medical transportation industry grew and changed with my former clients selling and retiring. Ambulance companies became "corporate" and a wave of consolidation began so the bigger ones could go public. To my benefit, a number of mid-level management guys (and gals) who did the daily operations and who knew me from my attorney days of representing their employers, began lining up to join my company. I hired them all and within three years, my ambulance company grew by over 200 percent.

Then came the next industry-wide audit.

Through its Medicare program, the federal government came up with a report that it was overcharged by various New York ambulance companies in the total amount of $109,000,000. My former government adversaries were on TV and quoted in the newspapers lambasting the ambulance services and alleging overpayment and fraud.

It made a lot of headlines and the eighteen named companies quickly looked over the list to see where they were in the pecking order. My company was number thirteen at $2,600,000.

Coincidently, as this became public, the national ambulance association was having its annual convention at the MGM casino in Las Vegas. All New York companies attended and we had a separate meeting to discuss this issue. The meeting was chaired by the ambulance owner who was number one on the list ($22 million) and he had the solution to our collective problems. He had contacts with a New York congressman who was in the process of running for the United States Senate.

If each company would contribute $25,000 to the congressman's future campaign, this problem would disappear. Yes, there might be some unknown token payment to settle, but the audit would go away. Make no mistake, it was not a bribe, but a legal campaign contribution to a concerned politician reviewing the entire situation and resolving it.

If I could take back just one moment of time; a second chance with twenty-twenty hindsight, it would be that day.

If there were the possibility to make a pact with the Devil to do it all over again—a chance to play back that one singular moment—I would have stood up, jumped on the dais, and screamed for the entire world to hear: "Damn the $25,000; let's give him $50,000."

Instead, I was horrified. I gave a speech, a lecture on right and wrong, the rule of law, and the fairness of our situation. The audit was bogus, illegal, and strictly a grandstanding bureaucratic tactic. "We don't need a politician," I recall saying. "We need justice."

To my everlasting regret, I refused to make that campaign contribution. It was the biggest mistake in my life.

Once I notified the Feds of my intention to challenge the audit, all hell broke loose. My company was accused of fraud and ripping off the Medicare system.

Medicare was able to temporarily suspend my company. Temporarily, as it turned out, was forever. Without Medicare reimbursement and with notice to all hospital and medical facilities of the potential fraud and abuse, my thriving company died overnight.

There are no words to adequately convey the fear when U. S. marshals arrive at your door with subpoenas to take all records and file cabinets, as well as your private papers. Boxes and boxes were taped shut and hauled out, all while my employees watched in indescribable horror as everything I once had disappeared.

A joint task force of state and federal workers spent the next three years looking over every single medical transport and the initial audit was expanded to five years. Every transaction was examined and re-examined.

I fought them—from hearing to hearing; from state to federal courts and appeals. It was a street fight, a legal war with guerrilla and nuclear tactics and weapons, with neither side giving an inch. It was a war of attrition.

That claim of $2,600,000? Even after expanding the audit two additional years, the final amount of overpayments was $4,920. Even the government dropped the allegation of fraud. That's less than a thousand dollars per year, or $82 per month. Put another way, a reduction of 99.7 percent over the initial claim.

The government claimed victory in the final ruling; after all, there was an overpayment of monies. They protected the taxpayers. They also reviewed every mailed or filed document to any government agency, looking for anything—and they found one. They claimed it contained false statements and since they were unsure as to who sent it—it was obviously a criminal conspiracy.

Such conspiracy by the owners and officers of the company (meaning my parents, brother, and wife) would be determined by a criminal trial. With separate attorneys to avoid any conflict of interest, the preliminary attorney fees quoted began at $250,000.

I was finished. I couldn't go on. Five years of hand-to-hand combat without any income had taken its toll. I gave up.

In March 2000, I pled guilty in federal court to a charge of submitting a false statement. Even with the government admission that there was no harm or monies obtained, it was a Class D felony. None of my family were ever implicated, but as the government pointed out, it was not a deal. It was also a coincidence that once I pled guilty, the government returned nearly $100,000.

I can say, however, that I am the only convict in New York who ever received a refund after pleading guilty. How's that for a lasting legacy? Let's be clear. I am not stating that I was framed or that there was a secret understanding. I pled guilty. I am and will forever remain a convicted felon. It is what it is ... pure and simple.

Am I bitter? I guess the honest answer is, " Not anymore." But I sure was.

I have realized, however, that it does not pay to be bitter or angry or resentful. Life goes on (whether you want it to or not) and looking back does not accomplish anything except making you ill. It's been nearly ten years—enough already.

Where does one pick up the pieces of his life after such a conviction? How does a family stay together after losing their home ... their lifestyle ... and after the shame and humiliation?

I've heard it said that when God shuts a door, He opens a window. I hope that's true.

Because if it is, then I guess I'm still going through that window. Maybe I gained a few pounds over the years, or that window may not be very large, but I do believe that such a window exists.

That window allowed me to keep my proudest accomplishment. I'm still with my wife and family. All our sons are with us in our new home state of Nevada.

I don't know how many families could survive what we went through. I don't know if it made us stronger, but I sure do know the meaning of love.

I learned that there is nothing like a crisis to discover who your friends are. Everybody likes you when you're successful and have money ... but it takes a very special individual; a true friend who stands by your side and watches your back when the bombs are incoming.

Let me remind you of another inspirational cliché—it's not whether you get knocked down, it's whether you get back up. Yes, I was knocked down—knocked completely out of the ring, as a matter of fact—but was able to stagger and eventually stand up again.

With the help of my family, business partners, and friends, we've established *The Vegas Voice*, the largest monthly senior newspaper in Nevada. With the economy being what it is and with newspapers in general dying by the day, I'm proud to say that our publication is still growing; still expanding.

And that's no small feat.

No, I never met Martha Stewart or George Steinbrenner who were able to successfully return to their original professions. However, I must admit that I love my life as publisher; working with my family and friends and meeting new people every day.

Maybe, just maybe, if I lose a few pounds and squeeze a little harder, I'll push through that window yet.

About the Author

Dan Roberts is the publisher and editor of *The Vegas Voice*, the most widely-read "Age 50+" monthly newspaper in Nevada. After moving to Las Vegas, Dan started the Medicare Advisory Foundation. This non-profit organization remains dedicated to representing and informing seniors of their Medicare and other health-related insurance benefits and rights.

In his previous life, Dan was an adjunct professor at Long Island University and was the general counsel and executive director for the New York State Ambulance Association, New York State Ambulette Association, and the New York State Medical Transportation Coalition.

Before his life collapsed in New York, he was president of an ambulance service that grew by over 200 percent and doubled the employee workforce within three years.

Despite the ups and downs of his life, Dan is still happily married and devoted to his childhood sweetheart, Amy. They have four sons.

Dan Roberts can be contacted at:
dan@thevegasvoice.net
Publisher/Editor, The Vegas Voice
2505 Anthem Village Drive, Suite E-513, Henderson, Nevada 89052
(702) 251-4441

A New Life

JENNIFER TARLIN

When I was hospitalized last summer, I swore to myself it would be the last time. As the paramedics entered my bedroom to take me to the ambulance for yet another ER visit, I felt the humiliation as it took five men to carry me down a flight of stairs. I was admitted to the hospital and given a diagnosis of the early stages of congestive heart failure. They gave me information on the disease and released me after a couple of days. I cried.

I have been severely overweight my entire life. As an adult, doctors categorized me as morbidly obese, defined as being one hundred or more pounds overweight. Since early childhood, I have been on multiple diets. I tried everything, but was not successful in losing weight. Each year I grew heavier, I became more hopeless. Eventually my body began to break down from years of obesity, and I developed serious health problems, such as type II diabetes.

I was hoping I would be able to lose this weight on my own, but after reading about weight loss surgery or bariatric surgery, I knew it was a last resort to save my own life. I researched the operation for nine years, finding the option that was best for me. I was willing to risk my life if this surgery could help me regain the life I had lost years ago. I was not ready to give up on myself.

About two years ago, I called around to the various insurance companies offered through my employer, and switched coverage at open enrollment. For medical necessity, most of the operation was covered, with only some out-of-pocket expense. I then found a surgeon and attended a seminar, the first step in the process. I completed a six-month diet with my internist, which was required by my insurance company, and completed all pre-operative testing. My information was submitted to the insurance, and I finally received a letter confirming my approval. My gastric bypass surgery was scheduled for October 27, 2008.

There are people who think weight loss surgery is the easy way out, but this could not be further from the truth. The reality is whether a person has gastric bypass or lap band surgery, this is only a tool; the rest is up to the patient to make a lifestyle change. People are quick to point out to me how often individuals regain the weight, but this is not going to be me. I have come too far.

Although it has not been an easy road, I have no regrets about making the choice to have the surgery. I have even inspired others to become healthier. My main reason for the surgery was to gain control over my diabetes. Two weeks post-op, I was off all medications, and my diabetes and health problems have been resolved. I no longer am a prisoner to insulin and I don't even monitor my blood sugar.

I changed my lifestyle, and now exercise daily. I enjoy going to the gym, in addition to hiking, swimming, and other activities. My entire life, I have had two dreams. One was to become athletic, and the other was to shop outside of the plus-sized department. Both of these have been achieved. I am now the healthy person I have always wanted to be. There will be no more ER visits for me. This December I am participating in my first athletic event, the Vegas Rock and Roll Marathon. Life is not passing me by anymore.

About the Author

Jennifer Tarlin is originally from the Boston area and has resided in Las Vegas for four years. She is a freelance writer, who has enjoyed writing since she was a child, writing her first story at the age of eight. She holds a B.A. in Journalism from the University of Massachusetts, Amherst.

After a lifetime of struggling with weight, she underwent gastric bypass surgery in October 2008, which has been a life-changing event. She would also like to embark on motivational speaking to bariatric patients in order to share her story to help others. A lifelong animal lover, she lives with her two precious cats, Tiffany and Margarita. She would like to dedicate this article to her beloved parents, Sheila and Harris Tarlin. Without their love and support, she would not be where she is today.

You can contact Jennifer Tarlin at:
jta1610622@aol.com
3243 Cheltenham Street, Las Vegas, Nevada 89129
(702) 606-2790

Challenge

The hardest choices we make in life are which bridges to cross and which to burn.

—David Russell

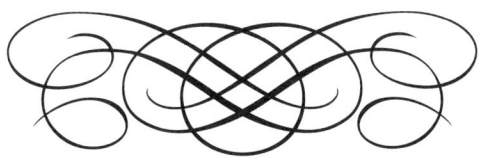

Playing the Hand You're Dealt

NANCY TODD

It was 3:15 in the morning, September 25, 2007, and I was spending yet another night sitting up in a plastic chair, in a hospital, watching over a sick son. With nothing but time on my hands, watching monitors change and flicker, I calculated how much of the last three years I'd spent in an ICU: a year, an entire year, an incredible 365 days.

I remember being pregnant with my first child, Hayden, and my and others' excitement about my impending membership into the "Motherhood Club." No one ever mentioned a darker aspect of that membership, the agony of a sick child, the fear of hospital admissions, the possibility of losing a child. Everyone talked of healthy children; no one mentioned those babies who struggle for the smallest achievement, sometimes, even for life itself.

Make no mistake, motherhood is the role dearest to my heart. By profession I'm a political consultant, a spin doctor, a hired gun, not as acerbic as James Carville or as capricious as Dick Morris, but still one whose chosen career has garnered many a name over the years and not all of them pleasant. In a traditionally male-dominated field, I am a woman who has lasted in this profession and now hold wide the door for other women to enter what once was an ABC ... an All Boys Club. I understand that uphill climb.

On college campuses across our nation, I've often spoken to young people about the political process and the need to be involved. I've talked to them about believing in themselves when no one else does, about overcoming tremendous obstacles and using naysayers for motivation. As a motivator and commentator on life, I've identified my rules for enduring: for example, I always have a "parachute" and always figure out why

Playing The Hand You're Dealt

the other guy is in the game. My standard closure is the admonition to be prepared to hit life's curve balls, since politics is an ever-changing challenge, with problems, surprises, and unexpected shifts from unexpected directions.

Politics is an extreme rollercoaster of life; at its essence, an intense, tumultuous sprint for some finish line with a term limit. Life, on the other hand, stretches before us like unending, rolling hills; the rises and falls of the rollercoaster are there, but, thankfully, disguised by the routine of daily living. The game is on, nevertheless, and the curve balls fly toward you, no matter your profession. I had my first child at thirty-six years of age, a pleasant but surprising reality in the early 90s. In 2002, I gave birth to full-term twins at forty-seven, a decidedly surprising curve ball, but doubly delightful.

Lincoln, one of the twins, was born with a heart condition called Tetrology of Fallot, one of those curves I knew nothing about until I had a child born with it, and then I learned it's fairly common in children born to mothers over forty. Lincoln is now seven, a veteran of six surgeries by the time he was three. Dr. Vaughan Starnes, a world-class pediatric heart surgeon at Children's Hospital in Los Angeles, cut through Lincoln's sternum and replaced his faulty heart valve in the first of these surgeries when he was only eight weeks of age.

A tiny doll-sized patient on the gurney, Lincoln breezed through the surgery, but the hospital, in an effort to increase his caloric intake prior to release, gave him a product, a powdered infant formula recalled by the FDA eight months prior. All powdered infant formulas had been labeled as suspect in April of 2002 (www.fda.org; April 11, 2002). Hospitals were never to give it to three classes of children: (1) low birth weight babies (Lincoln was 3.8 pounds at birth); (2) premature babies (Lincoln was on the cusp at thirty-eight weeks); and (3) babies with suppressed immune systems (Lincoln's severe heart condition definitely put him in this category.)

Powdered infant formula is not a sterile product, a fact the makers of this potentially deadly product do not want you to know. Healthy children can shake off the formula's load of bacteria, but the littlest of our species don't have a mature enough system to slough it off; instead, it eats through the intestines and releases e-coli through the body, often with fatal results.

I watched, alone, in the wee hours of a Sunday morning in September 2002 as Lincoln's heart rate climbed to 210 beats a minute (with 220 defined as cardiac arrest). In the middle of this "code blue" of doctors, wires, and machines, I crossed to Lincoln, secured a spot close to his head and leaned in. "Lincoln," I said, "I know you're thinking about going back and I don't blame you. You don't deserve all of this pain; you've done nothing wrong. Please stay, Lincoln, please. If you do, I promise you a spectacular life and a wonderful adventure." Slowly, his heart rate calmed. He spent eleven weeks in ICU, but as I knew he would, he made it. He beat the odds, just as he had when he was born.

The enterobacter (the result of the e-coli) erased his heart surgery benefits, and he had to have his valve replaced, again. This time we traveled to Stanford University where another world renowned surgeon, Frank Hanley, practices. The surgery succeeded, and expecting the normal seven-to-ten years from the valve, we traveled home. Unfortunately, Lincoln's valve didn't perform to standard, and one year later, when he turned three, we faced the knife again.

During this time in 2005, my fourteen-year-old son, Hayden, was diagnosed with leukemia, and another nightmare flared to life. We began aggressive treatment in Las Vegas with the only pediatric oncologist in the area. We learned that progress in the treatment of children's cancer has stood still since 1964, with no changes and no alterations. When asked why the usually progressive United States had managed no breakthroughs, the doctors admitted research in this area did not yield significant enough profit for the medical and pharmaceutical fields. The cancer market is significantly older.

Proceeding with the protocols available, after seven weeks, Hayden entered remission, and we breathed a sigh of relief, ultimately, for the remission, but also for the cessation of the daily horror and wrenching pain of the seven weeks of treatment. Our relief was short-lived, however; the doctor insisted on three more years of the protocol. I was watching Hayden's face as the doctor spoke. I saw the light leave his eyes, the dark stain of fear and dread erasing their bright twinkle. I immediately inquired about more humane options; the doctor, Dr B., told me I had no choice.

I'm an intelligent person, with rights, and a caring mother—and I don't believe in "no choice." I had read and learned all that I possibly could about leukemia, and my questions were on point, but the doctors had no answers, just the same protocol, no matter what effect or circumstances. Nor did the doctor look my child in the eye as he talked over him to a woman who, his tone indicated, should realize her place and unquestioningly follow his direction. He was incensed that I would question his judgment.

To enforce his point, the doctor immediately sued me, enlisting the assistance of Child Protective Services and the District Attorney. He painted me an unfit, irresponsible mother, with his proof that I had questioned his judgment. To make matters worse, Hayden's biological father, a Louisiana attorney who saw his son twice a year in twelve years of forced visitation, joined with the doctors in a sudden show of concern. He filed a "Friends of the Court" memo fighting his son and his son's mother in treatment options, and not allowing us to leave Las Vegas to find a more humane doctor and a more caring treatment. Learning his own father would act this way toward him, arbitrarily with no inquiry, no discussion, not even a visit, devastated Hayden.

Hayden and I trooped to court four times between May 2005, and July 2005, on this senseless charge. By the time the case was dismissed in July 2005, Hayden had relapsed from the stress and hassle, and the cancer had returned. The doctor couldn't wait to release us at this juncture and told me in the hospital corridor to "take Hayden home to die."

Hayden and I left immediately for Europe, bound for a clinic in Switzerland. We found humane treatment and a kind doctor who genuinely cared about Hayden and his treatment. We had discovered a home that treated my son as a patient and not as a protocol. We eventually moved to Germany where the doctors were doing some innovative procedures with viruses. We found a virus that ate the leukemic cells and saw an immediate turnaround in his cancer; the virus literally flipped the ratio of bad and good cells. We learned that the chemo necessary to bring the bad cells down enough to administer the virus used only

10 percent of the standard U.S. treatment for the same result, a relief to Hayden and a sobering validation of our opinion of the U.S. protocol administered by the Las Vegas doctor.

Our viral treatments reduced the cancer, and we were within striking distance of eradicating all of the bad cells. However, we couldn't stay to complete the treatment, as the four months while Hayden endured this rigorous treatment, Hayden's father, the only person who hadn't agreed to drop the charges against us, finally found a sympathetic judge in Las Vegas to mandate I return Hayden to the United States by October 25, 2005, or he would take custody of him. The issue of physical custody of Hayden, almost fifteen, didn't frighten me, but the medical custody by a man who would condemn my son to three years of an unwanted, torturous protocol overwhelmed Hayden and me, especially when we were experiencing such hopeful success in Germany. The judge also threatened to take my twins, Lincoln and his sister Sierra, now three years old and safe with my husband, unless Hayden and I returned immediately. We packed.

Hayden and I returned to Las Vegas on October 21, 2005, to address this case the following week with the plan to immediately return to Germany to finish our treatments. I was a genetic match for Hayden. My natural cancer-fighting cells were substituted for those destroyed in Hayden by the cancer and chemotherapy. The doctors in Germany took ten billion of my natural killer cells (NKcells) and increased them to fifty billion ten days later. They put them in Hayden with incredible results. We were to finish the last of the treatment and to do it once more to return Hayden to a cancer free life. Our court appearance took ten minutes to effect a complete dismissal of his father's weak and lingering case.

Unfortunately, on the trip to Las Vegas, Hayden caught a fungal infection in his port line (inserted in the chest to administer treatment), was admitted to the hospital, became critical, and died from the infection on November 21, 2005.

While Hayden was experiencing success in Europe, my second son, Lincoln, faced another heart surgery at the end of 2005. The surgery, scheduled for December 1, occurred five days after we buried his older brother. Although I could have delayed his surgery, Lincoln needed the heart valve replacement, and delaying it would not improve a dark and tragic year. For the third time in as many years, the doctors cracked Lincoln's chest and repaired his heart with a new valve, again with a proclaimed durability of seven-to-ten years.

I began 2006 with a determination to make good come from bad, to find a way to help others and give the struggle purpose. I fought through the pain. I struggled to live abundantly, giving my heart to my children, my family, my friends, and my work. It was a challenge.

By the end of 2006, Lincoln's heart valve failed again. His flow on the valve climbed above 50 percent and then escalated. The local cardiologists moved his checkups from every six months to every three months, always a sign, and not a good one. I prayed. My husband talked of returning to Stanford. I cringed at the thought of putting Lincoln through this horrific risk and pain again, and facing it possibly a dozen more times before he was grown. It was clear, though, that we couldn't continue without action. With each doctor visit, the failure was more evident and more threatening.

In June of 2007 I had a dream where I cried about Lincoln and the pain he would have to endure again. Hayden came to me in that dream and told me to look in England. I woke up the next morning a little dazed and more than curious about what was being done outside of the U.S.

My search revealed that Hayden was right. I was amazed to find that Dr. Philipp Bonhoeffer had created and patented a process where the heart valve could be replaced without surgery by entering through the femoral vein. I couldn't wait to see if we could replace Lincoln's valve that way. I reached out to political colleagues in Europe who promptly piqued the doctor's interest. I sent Lincoln's records, and three days later the doctor called with the magical words, "I believe I can help your son."

My husband, anxious about this procedure, felt it was too "outside the box." He wanted to wait until it was offered in the U.S. He worried that Lincoln's weight of thirty-seven pounds was too far below the previous successful surgical low of forty-five pounds. Not until we talked with Lincoln's cardiologists here in the states did my husband consent. The U.S. doctors were ecstatic and supported the new procedure wholly.

Life Choices: Navigating Difficult Paths

They had never understood why Lincoln's valves wore out so quickly and knew he faced another twelve or so of these dangerous surgeries before adulthood.

I told Dr. Bonhoeffer that Lincoln and I would be there the second he could see us. He graciously cleared his schedule for the following week. We took off. The MRI and other tests showed Lincoln's heart valve was working minimally, and we did not think Lincoln could last until his weight rose to the minimum weight of forty-five pounds. The doctor and I talked for several hours. We both needed to be comfortable and secure taking this big step together. We agreed that he would proceed, and if the vein proved too small or he felt the surgery too risky, he would stop. It was so nice to trust someone so much and to feel we were working together to help my son.

The procedure took place the following week, September 25, 2007, and it transpired without a hitch. Lincoln now has a new heart valve, one that works normally for the first time in his entire seven years. I spent the night at the hospital with him, of course. At 3:00 a.m. he began to rub his heart. I asked him if it hurt, and he said, "No, mom, but it sure feels different." I told him it worked; finally, it worked. Grateful for the darkness, I hid the tears in my eyes.

We flew back to the United States the next day, new heart valve in place and instructions to take a baby aspirin every day to avoid clotting. Lincoln left England without having his chest opened, with no pain, having experienced far less risk and danger, simply with an appointment for a yearly follow-up. I left England with my son's heart restored to normal function and with my own full of gratitude and thanks.

Yes, I'm lucky to be able to travel anywhere in the world to seek treatment for my sons' challenging medical conditions and diseases. I'm blessed to be able to afford these treatments. I know that. Long before I had any money, I was a citizen of this country, and I have always known it to be the greatest country in the world. In my travels I've been to many other countries, and nothing has shaken my faith and pride in living in the best of all countries. So, why can't we offer up-to-date medical care? Why do Americans have to slip off to Mexico to receive cancer treatments that work? Why do Americans have to fly to Switzerland to obtain chemotherapy that is 10 percent, a mere 10 percent, of what is prescribed here? Why do Americans give doctors and the FDA and the drug companies this power over our lives? Why are scare tactics the most predominant theme of cancer treatment in the greatest country in the world?

I made a difference in the lives of my children. Hayden experienced a transcendent hope and the climb to good health without the harsh protocol or awful side effects of the prescribed U.S. treatment of his disease. Without the reckless stubbornness of his biological father, he would have realized a medical cure. Lincoln's good health greets me every morning. I had the resources, and I acted for the best treatment for my children. People frequently ask me if I wonder "why me?" My thought is that I was blessed with three special souls who had a chance at life because I was their mother. I was fortunate to be able to play an integral role in tackling the challenges they faced.

They have made a significant difference in my life. What worries me now is how to make a difference for other mothers who sense or know that more humane and effective treatments are available, but don't have access to them. What worries me are the number of doctors in our country who do not want to be questioned and who demonstrate no desire to be on the cutting edge. What worries me are the people in our country who look upon doctors as godlike authorities whose verdicts are to be accepted as ultimate truths.

We can make a difference, and we can do it the old-fashioned American way of gaining and sharing knowledge and letting that knowledge empower us. We cannot let our medical care be only as good as our doctors, any more than we can let our country be only as good as our politicians. We must arm ourselves as citizens and protect our rights by demanding responsible care. The more we know, the stronger we become. The stronger we become, the fewer of our children will fall to complacent, self-satisfied health providers.

I tell this story to encourage you and to empower you. I ask that you believe in yourself, listen to your instincts, follow them, and ask questions. None of the treatments I discovered for my sons in Europe are allowed in the U. S. Betwcen the drug companies and the FDA, they probably never will be. We have precious few young men and women to lose to an uninspired health system and government agencies that exist to serve us as citizens. It is time to stand up for our children so that they may secure a better future for us all.

About the Author

Nancy Todd is a political consultant and president of Nancy Todd, Inc., an international strategic consulting firm based in Las Vegas, Nevada.

Todd cut her political teeth in Louisiana and since 1979 she has been a consultant to over 196 campaigns in forty-two states and six countries, with a winning record of 98 percent.

Treasurer of the board of directors of the International Association of Political Consultants and now past president and chairman of the American Association of Political Consultants, Todd was inducted into the prestigious Hall of Fame of the AAPC in March 2008, the first woman to be so honored. Her articles and commentary have appeared nationally in newspapers and professional publications.

She is a frequent speaker both nationally and internationally for governments, heads of state, key leaders in emerging democracies, and major universities including Harvard, the John F. Kennedy School of Government, George Washington University, Georgetown University, and Vanderbilt University.

Nancy Todd can be contacted at:
nltodd@aol.com
www.NancyTodd.com
9030 W. Sahara Avenue, Suite 455, Las Vegas, Nevada 89117
(702) 838-0642

Finding My Purpose

AIMMEE KODACHIAN

Have you ever asked yourself, What's my purpose? We are all born with special powers that give us the ability to achieve anything we want.

In 2005, I was driving on the freeway, having just finished with a business meeting that went very well. I was feeling awesome. All of a sudden, I just felt so overwhelmed with good feelings, all kinds of emotions, like they were coming out of my skin. I started to feel tears running down my face. I heard all this honking and realized I was slowing down the freeway traffic. I took the first exit I saw, pulled over, and broke down crying. These weren't tears of sorrow or sadness. They were tears of joy. I couldn't believe I had done it!

It was at that exact moment when I realized that my purpose was to share my story—the story of hope—no matter what the cost! Instead of going to my next meeting, I started my car and drove home. I dropped everything I was doing. I mean everything; my business and social calendar. I decided if I was going to do this, I had to give 100 percent of my energy, time, and money in order to write the story. I felt that was my *purpose* in life. I promised myself right then and there that I would follow my heart. This is where *Tears of Hope*, my true life story was born. Let me share with you some of the story.

I was born and raised in Lebanon, a small country in the Middle East. I always struggled in school. Every time I tried to read I saw the letters jumping off the page at me. I was punished and labeled as stupid. Not just by my schoolmates but by teachers as well. I was held back year after year.

The kids in my class didn't want to play with me because I looked very different from them; I was much taller and older than they were.

Finding My Purpose

The kids my age didn't want to play with me because they thought something was wrong with me, and they reminded me of that every chance they got. My teachers and family members thought I was just plain lazy.

I knew I wasn't lazy. I also knew, at a very young age, that I wanted to become a teacher so I could help others not to feel the way I felt. Surely, there was a better way to get children to understand how to read and write than punishment and humility.

It wasn't until much later in life that I discovered I had a learning disability. Today we know it as dyslexia. It wasn't the average kind of dyslexia; it was the kind where you hold your book upside down and it will take you a few seconds to realize it.

In 1975, I was twelve years old when the Lebanese Civil War began. We were one of the first families to become homeless. I lost my closest brother right before my eyes. The tragedies were numerous and seemed never ending. The war affected our community in every way. Not only were we losing our homes and family members, we were losing our businesses and jobs. The bombings affected our utilities like water and electricity. It didn't take long before our streets were so riddled by bombings, they were useless to use as transportation for food or to take us to shelter. Going back and forth to school was impossible. The combination of my dyslexia and the war was the beginning of many challenges and the end of my schooling. I was in the fourth grade So much for being a teacher!

For thirteen years I lived through the war. I had to learn to keep my fear in balance in order to stay focused. I was lucky enough to escape death three times. My family struggled to stay together, but my mother soon realized she couldn't raise me. She didn't have the financial or emotional resources. My soon-to-be husband convinced my family he could give me a better life and exactly three days after my fourteenth birthday, my mother persuaded me to get married. By fifteen, I was the proud mother of a beautiful baby girl named Silva. Before I turned eighteen, my husband decided the pressure of the war, being a husband, and father was just too much to handle so he fled the country leaving me with no money, skills, or education, and a precious child to care for.

Life Choices: Navigating Difficult Paths

I had nowhere to go but back to my family who couldn't provide for me before. Now I was coming back and bringing another mouth to feed as well. I can't tell you how many times I was told I couldn't make it. Most people around me told me to give my baby to my husband's family. I refused as I knew no one could take better care of her than me. I didn't know how I was going to do it, but I absolutely knew in my heart that I could.

In 1988, I was in my twenties and fortunate enough to get the opportunity to come to the United States, to the best country in the world, the land of opportunity. As you know, I had no skills or education. I had a young daughter to raise. On top of all that, I didn't even speak English. It didn't take me long to realize that I was faced with a different kind of fear. I admit ... I was scared. I felt alone even though I had the power of hope this country offered me. After all, it wasn't only a new country, it was a new way of living.

I had come to the U.S. on a visa with no plans or accommodations. I had a few family members here who I knew truly wanted to help me but didn't know how. Everyone had their own lives and having two more people around wasn't easy on them. We were a mother and daughter with not much hope and even fewer options. Everyone said we would not make it here, but I wasn't going to let my spirit be crushed. I took the very first job I was offered and was happy to be making $3.00 an hour. I felt rich. I soon realized that if I was going to make any kind of life for my daughter and myself, my first priority had to be to learn the language.

This was the beginning of my journey to success, which brings me to 2005 when I made the decision to write my book. I met with loads of criticism and again was told I couldn't do it. I was reminded often that I could barely write an entire sentence, let alone a whole book. Yet, I felt deep down in my heart and soul that sharing my story was my purpose. I wasn't going to allow anything to stop me ... I mean anything. I wrote the book.

Before long I realized that books didn't have legs. I had to find a way to get the message out. I remember my first interview on public radio. I had learned to speak English and thought I was ready for the

Finding My Purpose

interview, but when the host started asking me questions, I froze up. I couldn't find the words to form the sentences quickly enough to answer his questions. He was so sharp and professional. He did all he could to make me feel comfortable during the interview. Writing about my story was a whole different ballgame than talking about it. Here I thought I was not going to let anything stop me. I thought that writing the book was the hard part. I was wrong. Not only was I struggling with the language, I still had my Middle Eastern mentality. I started feeling the pressure of my culture telling me I was not supposed to share my story with anyone, let alone the world.

I suppose I could have let that interview be the end of my journey. I was walking down the hallway out to my car when my cell phone rang. It was my daughter, Silva, calling to let me know she was very concerned about me since she listened to the interview. She let me know that I sounded very uncomfortable and she was concerned with how I was going to deliver my message. I let my daughter know that I appreciated her concern, but I knew in my heart I was living my purpose. I told her not only was I going to keep on interviewing, I was going to become a motivational speaker. The words were out of my mouth before I even realized I had said them aloud. I could picture her head shaking. I knew I wasn't going to let anything stop me from living my purpose and fulfilling my passion to help others. I couldn't allow myself to be embarrassed by my weaknesses. I was very proud of my strengths.

We get strength from many different sources. As an author, your readers can strengthen you like no others. I remember receiving several letters from readers and I'd like to share one that is still special to me today:

> Dear Aimmee,
>
> *Tears of Hope* was a God-sent gift that I will always cherish and I wanted to personally thank you for inspiring me to love, forgive, and to live life to the fullest each and every day, because tomorrow is not promised. My mother and I have been estranged for almost four years and after reading your book, I now realize that nothing is more important than forgiveness and

love. When I read the chapter where you forgave your mother and sister-in-law even after how they mistreated you over the years, I was overwhelmed with peace and understanding that even those close to you, who have hurt you, need healing. When we can forgive we can heal.

I read *Tears of Hope* in just one day and I had to write you and tell you that it has been a life-changing event for me. You are truly an amazing woman with extraordinary patience and love for your family. Your passion and purpose gives inspiration to all women, of all different ethnic backgrounds, that God is the way and the answer.

God Bless
Cathy Steen, Irvine, CA

We deal with obstacles almost every day. Especially when we try to live our purpose, we start to feel the pressure of outside forces. The reward you'll get from living your purpose gives you an almost euphoric feeling that is hard to put into words. There is joy, happiness, excitement, delight, exhilaration … all those and more rolled into one.

Remember how I wanted to become a teacher someday? That was a dream back then and today it's a reality. Although I'm not a teacher in the traditional sense, I now have the opportunity to reach and touch thousands of people through my speaking. There was no magic pill. It took effort and persistence to turn my obstacles into opportunities. If in your heart and soul you know something is your purpose, don't let anyone or anything stop you. Whenever you hear yourself or someone else tell you "No, you can't," tell yourself, "Yes, I can! I have choices."

About the Author

Aimmee Kodachian is a middle-eastern Armenian woman, who authored *Tears of Hope*, an inspiring true story that recounts the many tragedies she faced while living through the Lebanese Civil War. Aimmee overcame obstacles and learned to stay focused by drawing on her inner strength and seeing opportunity in the enormous adversities she endured.

Today, Aimmee is a faculty speaker for iLearningGlobal.tv, which brings together the world's top educators, teachers, and speakers. Her passion for helping others drives her to continuously work on exciting projects which allow her to use her unique talent to give people hope and guide them to the realization that even during the most difficult times of their lives, they can have peace within their hearts and minds.

Aimmee Kodachian can be contacted at:
Aimmee@LivingMotivated.com
www.LivingMotivated.com
www.ilearningglobal.biz/learning
www.ilearningglobal.tv
(702) 545.5891

Experience

Destiny is no matter of chance. It is a matter of choice. It is not a thing to be waited for, it is a thing to be achieved.

—William Jennings Bryan

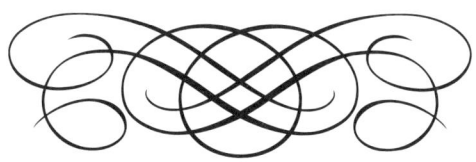

Why Not?

ANNE ABERNATHY

In February 2006, I found myself preparing to carry the flag in the Opening Ceremonies for an unprecedented sixth Winter Olympic Games appearance all because I never stopped asking, 'Why not?'

I had no idea I was going to be an Olympic athlete. When I was growing up, women were not even supposed to participate in sports. My mother was from the old genteel South and in her mind sports were just not ladylike. Still I always pressed the issue with Mom by asking, "Why not?"

In the early 1980s, I discovered luge on a ski trip in Lake Placid, New York. Ironically, the trip was my mom's idea. My mother was afraid that her only daughter, who at the time did not have a steady boyfriend, was never going to fall in love and settle down. Using her own unique brand of logic, she decided that presenting me with a Christmas gift of a weekend co-ed ski trip by bus would do the trick. Never mind the fact that I would have to fly from my home in St. Thomas, Virgin Islands to Washington D.C. only to jump on a bus for a twelve-hour drive with complete strangers to Lake Placid, New York. But I was game and thought, 'Why not?'

Unfortunately, the skiing conditions at Lake Placid were dismal; the slopes were pure ice. So when someone suggested that we go over and watch the bobsled training, the response was automatic: "Why not?"

Everyone knew what bobsled was because the Olympic Winter Games had just been held there in 1980. We watched a bobsled come down the track with four guys in it, slamming the walls left and right. They wore shoulder pads and helmets and were coming down the track with their heads between their knees and I thought this can't be fun—these guys are nuts, absolutely nuts!

Then I saw a sign that said "This way to the luge track" and thought what the heck is loogie? No one was quite sure how to pronounce it. Although it was an Olympic sport, it was not one that had been featured during the Olympic broadcasts. We followed the signs and walked up just as a luge athlete went flying by. After watching the noisy bobsleds banging down the track, the luge seemed like it was just floating by at an incredible speed. How cool!

There were about twenty of us gathered beside the track. A luge coach standing up on the track wall asked anyone who wanted to try it to take a step forward. Immediately, eighteen people took a step back. There I stood, along with a lone fireman from Maryland. While we hadn't taken a step back, we hadn't actually stepped forward either. We slowly turned and looked at each other and said, "Why not?"

Little did I know that by not taking a step back, I was choosing to begin a journey into the Olympic record books. Luge became my passion. After my first run down the track, I was hooked. My poor mother was hoping I would find true love on that ski trip to New York. I did fall in love, but it was with luge. Much to her chagrin, I would remind Mom years later that my entry into the sport of luge was actually all her fault.

I started a vigorous training program and traveled to the luge tracks throughout Europe for practice. But before I had even raced in an international competition, my Olympic dream was almost shattered. I was diagnosed with cancer. This was before the days of Olympians like Magic Johnson and Lance Armstrong who entered the Games with a history of HIV and cancer respectively. At this time, any athlete with a serious medical condition was considered damaged goods and never had a chance to qualify.

One of my doctors told me not to train any more.

"Why not?"

He said, "You need to focus on getting well."

"My job is to get to the Olympics; your job is to get me well!" was my immediate response.

On my next medical visit I noticed a different attitude from doctors and staff. I was no longer the Cancer Victim, but instead the Olympic Hopeful. They became part of my team with an Olympic goal, not just a medical one. Our perseverance and dedication paid off when the cancer went into remission and I qualified for the 1988 Calgary Winter Olympic Games.

At my first Olympics in Calgary, while I was taking my last two official training runs, the announcers were practicing their commentating in German, French, and English—the three official languages of the Olympic Games. When I returned to the start house after my first run, my coach from Austria and Georg Hackel, an athlete from Germany, were laughing. My coach told me that they had just announced that I was Dreiundreizig (thirty-three in German).

I said. "Yea, so?"

He said, "Your German is not so good; you are Dreiundzwanzig."

I said, "No, your English is not so good, I'm thirty-three."

He said, "twenty-three."

I said, "thirty-three."

Then he said, "You're thirty-three? That's older than me!"

I said, "That's your problem, not mine."

I looked at Georg, who by this time was literally rolling on the floor of the start house laughing.

I said, "What's so funny?"

He stood up put his hands on his hips and said, "You can't luge."

I said, "Why not?"

Georg answered, "You're too old to luge!"

I just stared at him and said, "I wasn't five minutes ago."

In Germany when you turned thirty your sports career was automatically over. You weren't supposed to luge after the age of thirty, but no one had ever told me that.

Five Olympics later in the 2002 Salt Lake City Games, Georg came up to me and said he owed me a beer. I looked him straight in the eye and said the entire German women's luge team owed me a keg! George had just won his fifth Olympic medal and the German women's team had swept the luge medals, yet they were all older than I was in my first Olympics when I was declared too old to luge.

Without realizing it, I was able to break a barrier for these Olympic medalists who would have been passed by because someone had arbitrarily determined a mandatory retirement age.

In January 2001, just a year before the 2002 Olympics, I was in the top-seeded group when I had a devastating crash during a World Cup race in Altenberg, Germany. The crash left me unconscious for over twenty minutes. I was told that I'd never be able to drive a car again, much less compete in the Olympics twelve months away. Once again I was told, "Don't train;" prompting my "Why not?" response.

I was determined to find a way. My team osteopath and I temporarily relocated to California for four and-a-half months. There, among other rehab regimens, I underwent brain biofeedback therapy twice a day, five days a week. The therapy basically meant playing video games with my brainwaves; no joystick, just wires connected to my head. As my gameplay improved, so did the symptoms of my head trauma.

Physical training took a back seat to biofeedback therapy. It was all I could do to get back on the race circuit. Once again, hard work and perseverance paid off and just four weeks before the Olympic Opening Ceremony, I qualified for my fifth Olympics.

This time, however, I realized that it wasn't as important to be in the top ten; the important thing was that I was there. I had overcome, and set a new Olympic record as the oldest woman to ever compete in the Winter Olympic Games in the process. I had already won because I was there.

Setting my sights on the 2006 Olympics in Torino, Italy was a difficult decision. It would be a tough road, both physically and financially. Aside from that, I was already in the record books, so I wasn't sure what it would accomplish.

While pondering the decision, I was invited to speak at a Red Hat Society convention. The Red Hat Society is a social group primarily for women over the age of fifty who, aside from wearing red hats, congregate merely to have fun. During my speech I told the audience that if I did compete in the upcoming Olympics, I would have to wear this ...

Life Choices: Navigating Difficult Paths

and pulled out a red helmet from the podium. There was an immediate standing ovation.

Following my talk, I was surrounded by women who wanted to help me 'Slide for Six' in 2006. Returning home, there was a message on my answering machine from a woman who had heard my speech. She simply said, "What do we have to do to get your butt to the Olympics?"

I was in the unique position to be the first woman over fifty to qualify for the Winter Olympic Games and I truly loved to luge, so why not?

That's how in February 2006, I found myself standing with 2000 other Olympians outside the Torino Olympic stadium preparing to march in the opening ceremony parade of athletes.

What an emotional experience. As we started slowly moving towards the stadium, I couldn't help but reflect on my journey. Most people dream of being at the Olympics; I was there not once, not twice, but as the first woman to participate six times in the Winter Games. Many of my fellow Olympians were not even born when I started in the sport.

We entered the arena and as I proudly waved the flag, one announcer introduced me to the world by my nickname, Grandma Luge. Immediately another commentator changed it on the spot and dubbed me Grandma Olympia. I could only smile and think, 'Why not?'

About the Author

Anne Abernathy, nicknamed Grandma Luge, an unlikely, courageous athlete from the Virgin Islands overcame a series of hardships including cancer, head trauma, broken bones, fourteen knee surgeries, and even a hurricane that destroyed her home to become the first six-time female Winter Olympian.

She is the oldest woman to qualify for the Winter Olympics, setting records and breaking barriers along the way. In the 1992 Lillehammer Games, Anne became the first Olympian to create an online diary. During the Albertville Games, she was first to compete with a camera on board, a feat that earned an Emmy nomination.

From the Pentagon to the House of Parliament to Fortune 500 companies, she is in demand as an enlightening and highly entertaining speaker. Her appearances include the *Today Show*, the *Tonight Show*, *Good Morning America*, *MSNBC*, *Fox Sports Radio*, and the Discovery Channel.

She's a Guinness world record holder whose passion, unique wit, and wisdom will inspire YOU to step up, find the fire within and just do it—why not?

Anne Abernathy can be contacted at:
DuPlain International Speakers
Jan@duplain.com
AAnne@aol.com
www.grandmaluge.com
(202) 486-7004 — (866) DUPLAIN — (703) 863-9697

The Best of You

ELLE SWAN

Choose.

Choosing is the most important factor in living a healthy life. The condition of your body, at this very moment, is a direct result of your willingness to choose.

Acting on this simple but profound truth will allow you to expand further and further into the life you've always wanted. You will no longer be a slave to bad habits and you will no longer need to defend them. Imagine what it would be like to lose weight and break any addiction once and for all. I learned the hard way, but you can make a different choice right here, right now.

If you had been a fly on the dingy desperate walls of my world in the 90s, you would zigzag through chaos, confusion, and decay. You would quickly choose to fly away and escape the swat of death that was closing in around me. If I could have, I would have done the same. A five-year series of toxic choices slowly melted my drive and ability to jump to safety. The toil of exponential depression made it okay to live in an abandoned van with strangers, despite having a private college degree.

Based on America's growing rate of preventable illness, obesity, and dependency on prescription drugs, it's a good bet that the walls of your life could use a little cleaning. What would I see if I were a fly on your wall? What part of you is melting away?

I'll go first. My obvious problem was alcohol. In the beginning of that five-year spiral, it made everything I did sensational. A few glasses of wine or a couple of martinis would dissolve my shyness and place me center stage. Like the great historical literary talents, a glass of scotch seemed to make my time at the computer more creative. Then there was must-have mimosas at Sunday brunch and the hot toddy that made the winters in New York so much more bearable.

Yes, it was all so quaint … in the beginning.

Then it became progressively worse. We often think that gravity only affects us physically, but hindsight has taught me that you will one day be faced with the gravity of your decisions. Or should I say the gravity of your choices.

There were warning signs all along my fall into darkness. Like most people, I looked the other way. One of the first signs was the fact that I always made sure I had alcohol in my house. It was as necessary as toothpaste, paper towels, or laundry detergent. The best part was I, like most people, could purchase all of my "necessities" from the same store. This was a very convenient way to lose control without ever noticing. Yet, losing control was the best thing that could have ever happened to me. It expedited my demise and prevented me from dragging my self-destructive behavior into this decade.

In case you are wondering, I will not end this story without supplying you with a glimpse of my lowest point. But I would be doing us both a disservice if I gave the impression that this story was only about me.

The most important person at this very moment is you. What happens to you, from this point forward, is far more important than everything that ever happened to me. My hope is that you will choose to benefit from my tragic fall.

It is not necessary to become estranged from your family, ruin your promising career, end up cold, hungry, and alone. No, you can choose health and vibrant living right now. Or you can fool yourself into thinking that making healthy choices, every now and then, is just as good. Don't be foolish.

The next sign of danger manifested in my internal world. Gloom crept up on me like a kicked-over can of grey paint, covering me slowly but steadily. My natural-born optimism was shifting into "half empty" thinking. No matter what I did, I couldn't make happiness last. The darkness that ultimately became the end of this story hadn't consumed me, so I could hide it from those around me. But inside, life was becoming increasingly bleak, pointless, and grey.

Life Choices: Navigating Difficult Paths

I decided I needed another drink. For you, it may be another piece of cake, an anti-depressant, or a cigarette...anything to quiet that icky feeling. The problem is that it never quite works, does it? A few minutes of relief here and there, maybe even an hour or two. No matter how hard you try to hide, that grey is still in your tracks.

What I really needed was to choose to clean myself up. But that would have been too much of a hassle. What about you?

Day after day, the gravity of my choices made cleaning up seem utterly impossible. I mean, who has the time for all that? I was too busy mustering up the energy to make it through another day. I was too busy trying to remember what happened the night before and trying to get the next gig to pay my bills. Sound familiar?

The third sign was isolation. I began to isolate in my house. The less I was around other people the better. I'd go out, do what I needed to do, and retreat to my grey cocoon. Everyone around me was either pushed away or walked away, including my entire family. I even diagnosed myself as "a loner" to rationalize my newfound need to be separate and have disregard for others' feelings. If this sounds like you, take it from me, you are choosing to get worse … not well. Of all the choices I made during those ugly five years, isolation was absolutely the most dangerous.

The fourth sign accosted me in a full-length mirror. My natural-born optimism had disappeared. Who was this heavier, gloomy version of me? Instead of answering this question truthfully, I decided to limit my time in front of full-length mirrors. It felt better to avoid looking at me, so I created a new truth for myself. From then on, the size I was didn't matter and I didn't care. This was the most blatant warning that I had a problem and I chose not to see it.

Instead, I had another drink.

Then the signs stopped coming. As my grandmother would say, "Grace runs out." God never turns his back on us, but there is definitely a reason why he gave us free will. We have been given a choice. We can heed the signs or we can lose our way and our peace of mind. Self-will is a very deceptive instrument. It is the curse of becoming an adult and claiming the right to do whatever we want to do.

My self-will turned against me and left me stranded on the highway of life with no hope and no options. It will take many pages and many years to contextualize the painful and totally avoidable details of those years, but as promised, here's a glimpse:

I clamored my way from the east coast to the west coast, city by city, as if I was being pulled to this very moment in time. With no clear destination in mind, I rolled forward, place to place, like a raggedy tumbleweed. I ended up in the Bay Area for a while, until the house where I was staying was raided. We were all sitting around doing what addicts and alcoholics do when all of a sudden the front door came crashing in. There was a blur of policemen slamming everyone around and smashing wrists in cuffs.

With all the madness that had become routine for me, I had never been to jail. Almost everyone I met along the way had been many times so I stood resolved waiting for my turn. One of the officers grabbed me with his eyes and then motioned to a back door.

I ran until I couldn't run anymore. Then I walked and walked and walked. I could feel that there was no help on the way and none of the people I passed cared about my tears. I had gotten my wish. I was finally all alone, and now I was wishing for jail.

My hero was a prostitute named Sylvia. She came walking out of a yard at the very moment I crossed by the gate. Our feet just fell into the same flow and she asked me where I lived.

"Nowhere," I told her.

"Nowhere? Wow. I don't believe I've ever heard that before."

"Well, it's true."

"So where you going?" she asked.

"I don't know," I said, as I started to cry.

Sylvia was Caucasian and much much older than I. Although she was just as dusty-looking as me, when she put her arm around my shoulder and said, "You'll be alright," I knew there was a time in her life when she had made the same statement to a child of her own.

"We don't live too far from here; I'm sure it will be okay if you stay for a while."

I really had no expectations of what her place would be like and, to be honest with you, it didn't even cross my mind to pass judgment when we walked up to the broken down van that Sylvia and her two friends called home. I simply climbed in and made peace with the lesser version of myself and the culminating truth of my choices.

My entire platform as an author and speaker is the result of what happened in that van. I learned that people are having "van" experiences in the comfort of their own homes. Some live alone but many have the company of "lesser" friends (or family members.) They see you living less than your best and they tell you that you will be alright. You stay the same and so do they until you all look up and notice that nothing stays the same. You have simply gotten worse together.

You may be tempted to think that I am comparing you with Sylvia and me. If so, that is a mistake. Real friends will encourage you to do what is best for you even if it means you will go away. Sylvia was that kind of woman.

One day, I begged her to take me with her and show me how to be a prostitute. Reluctantly she agreed. She told me I would never get picked up without makeup so we walked to a very popular grocery store. We picked the colors that would work for me and when no one was looking we put them in our pockets.

After walking a few blocks, we stopped in an empty parking lot and sat down on the curb. I quickly began applying my makeup, super eager to learn my new trade. Sylvia noticed my excitement and snatched blush and brush out of my hand. She smashed them in the street and began to scream at me.

"You don't want this! You don't want this life! Look at me ... I'm fifty-two years old living on the streets. You-don't-want-to-end-up-like-me!"

In a very odd and unusual way, Sylvia was begging me to make better choices for myself. She was saying, "Learn from my experience."

I invite you to learn from mine. Make the choice now to be a better you!

About the Author

You will never be comfortable with your daily excuses after working with Elle Swan. She is a Vibrant Living Expert who transcended the darkness that destroys most people … forever.

At her lowest moment in life, she was overweight, addicted to alcohol, homeless, and left for dead.

Elle's remarkable journey from depression and deprivation, to vibrancy and abundance, ignited a passion inside her that illuminates the lives of all who cross her path. She is a master at identifying and transforming self-defeating habits. You can overcome them! Elle Swan will show you how.

As an author, speaker and coach, she reveals her cutting-edge methods for Vibrant Living in a variety of health, image, and wellness products and services.

Elle Swan can be contacted at:
www.elleswan.com
Visit the website for ways to eliminate the "dark spots" in your life TODAY.

What Was I Thinking?
Confessions of an Avid Adventurer

BOB WALKER

In the summer of 1983, life was good. I was a salvage diver and lived on my thirty-two-foot salvage boat, Retriever, in Avalon Harbor on Catalina Island. Located twenty-six miles off the southern California coast, Catalina Island was properly dubbed the "Island of Romance" in a song made famous by the Four Preps in the late 1950s.

During the time I lived on the island, a woman diver I knew, I'll call her Sue, told me about an underwater tunnel that ran about fifty yards through Long Point, a piece of land that jutted out from the island into the sea, located five miles up the island's coast from Avalon. The tunnel's existence had long been the topic of barroom conversations among divers. Sue claimed to know where the tunnel was. She also claimed to have made the trip through it.

We made the "what-were-we-thinking" choice to take a stab at the tunnel and on a sunny afternoon loaded our dive gear aboard my boat and motored up the island's coast. Anchoring just off Long Point, we slipped into our gear and swam to shore, where we climbed up the rocky outcropping. It took an hour of determined searching to find the access hole twenty feet above the high tide line. We stood for several minutes, looking down into the hole that was no more than four feet across and dropped twenty feet straight down until water lapped at the edges.

We had a choice to make. Would we jump into the hole with only one way out? Or would we be overcome by common sense and our instincts for survival and return to the bar?

You guessed it. Consumed by the adrenaline rush and without much thought or planning, I stepped off the edge and plunged into the water below. When the bubbles cleared, I was in an underwater cave that had an opening on one side. Sue soon joined me. We had already decided that I would lead, and the tunnel seemed large enough to get through, so I headed in. The walls of the tunnel were decorated with a myriad of different colored sea life. There were bright purple sea anemones, rusty red coral, and dark purple, almost black, spiny sea urchins. As I swam deeper into the tunnel the ambient light dimmed and I turned on my underwater flashlight.

After what could have been no more than fifty feet, the tunnel narrowed dramatically until I could no longer swim. The tunnel had silted in and I had to crawl along the bottom. I moved slowly, searching ahead with the beam of my underwater light until the scuba tank on my back scraped the top of the tunnel and became tangled in rocks and sea plants.

I was stuck thirty feet under water in a dark tunnel! I twisted and turned, trying to free the tank and hoses, but nothing I did would free me from the death grip of the roof of the tunnel. I checked my air gauge and found that my panicky thrashing was causing me to burn through my air supply at an alarming rate. I had another choice to make. I could either continue to thrash and fight the tunnel or I could stop and think and figure it out like I had in other tight spots.

I took several minutes to calm myself and get my breathing under control before I managed to work myself free and back out of the tunnel. Sue and I surfaced in the small hole where we had entered the water and concluded there was no way to climb back up. We had made a bad choice in entering the water and now our choices were limited to just one. The only way out was to force our way through the narrowed tunnel to open water on the other side of the point.

I knew the tunnel was impassable with the air tank on my back so I removed it in the cave and pushed it ahead of me when I re-entered the tunnel. When I arrived at the spot where I had become hung up, I took several deep breaths, removed the air regulator from my mouth, and pushed the air tank into the narrow tunnel. I squeezed and wiggled my way through the next ten feet until the tunnel widened again. I reclaimed my air supply and settled down in a larger chamber to wait for Sue.

She had a tougher time of it. My struggles had stirred up the bottom silt and, even with her powerful underwater light, the visibility was zero. She waited until she heard me tap three times on my air tank with the butt of my knife. That was our signal that I had made it through and it was okay for her to follow.

Sue took a lot longer to work her way through the narrow slot and became disoriented from a lack of oxygen, having been without her air supply for well over two minutes. In her confusion, she could not find her air regulator and panic set in. I shared my air supply with her until I located her regulator, cleared it, and re-inserted it in her mouth.

We settled in the larger chamber and assessed our options. If we went forward, we would have to navigate another hundred feet of tunnel in unknown conditions. We had no way of knowing if the rest of the tunnel was blocked or not. If we returned, we knew we could arrive at the hole where we had entered and have a limitless supply of air and light. Someone would eventually notice the anchored boat and come looking for us. Would anyone think to look for us in a sink hole that had taken us an hour to find? Would they write us off as having drowned and disappeared in the open sea near the anchored boat? We had another choice to make. Did we want to become victims and hope to be rescued or could we find our own way out? I've always found that if I waited for help, I put myself at the mercy of other people's choices. Sometimes help came, sometimes it did not. The choice we made would be life or death. Did we wait or did we take action? Both choices had the potential to go either way.

Through a series of hand gestures illuminated only by our underwater flashlights, we decided our only real choice was to take action and continue through the tunnel to the other side. Had we known what lay ahead, we might have chosen to return to our starting point and wait for the help that might or might not arrive.

As we proceeded through the tunnel, we had to squeeze through two more places, one of which was even narrower than the first. My nerves were raw and my mind wandered. We didn't have enough air left to return the way we had come. The only way out was to continue into the unknown.

Forty-five minutes into our dive, I spotted light literally at the end of the tunnel and paused to again check my air supply. Of the 3,000 pounds of air I had when we started the dive, I was down to less than 250 pounds. If we didn't get to the surface in the next five to six minutes, the air would run out and I'd be sucking dents in my tank. At only thirty feet under water I could usually stretch a tank full of air up to seventy-five minutes, but the stress had taken its toll on my breathing control. I didn't know how much air Sue had, but it had to be about the same as mine.

I continued on until I was within five feet of the opening and could see the kelp waving at me, inviting me to the clear water outside the tunnel. Then I saw our last obstacle ... the head of an enormous Moray eel. This guy was the largest Moray I'd ever seen. He appeared to be poised for attack, his six-foot plus length undulated and his head took aim at my air tank. Almost out of air, I had no option except to confront the eel head-on. Thankful that the tank led the way, I pushed it through the opening and the Moray struck at it twice. Not able to get a grip on the tank, the eel shot forward and sank his stiletto-like teeth into the web of my glove between my thumb and fingers. He twisted and pulled until the glove came free and he slithered away into deeper water taking his prize with him. I gave a couple of kicks of my fins and was out of the tunnel with Sue trailing close behind.

We rose together to the surface and rested, relieved to again see the deep blue sky and breathe the sweet sea air tinged with the pungent smell of kelp slumped on the nearby rocks. Our adventure was over. When the sun dropped behind the island, we leisurely kicked our way back to the boat.

Life is a series of choices. Some are good, some not so good, and some fall into the category of "what in the world were we thinking?" We had made a terrible choice to enter the tunnel, but we had survived through the other choices we made.

About the Author

Bob Walker is a man of high adventure who squeezes every drop of excitement from each day. He has been a salvage diver, Alaska fishing guide, lobster fisherman, skydiver, and performed fish feeding shows under Catalina Island's glass bottom boats. But he's not just an adventurer. Bob's been a CEO and now works with organizations to provide immediate practical solutions to management and team problems that involve communication, conflict, and ineffective performance. Bob teaches proven real-world strategies that can be used in the trenches, where the real work takes place.

Bob is a true problem solver. He has coached others to excellence and authored the book, *Sink or Swim Problem Solving*.

bobwalker4@cox.net
www.sinkorswimproblemsolving.com
33152 Acapulco Drive, Dana Point, CA 92629
(949) 290-2020

Spirituality

Our choices in life are made according to our sense of our own worth.

—Kaylan Pickford

An Enacted Miracle: Who Heals the Healer?

GINETTE OSIER BEDSAUL

There are two ways to live: you can live as if nothing is a miracle; you can live as if everything is a miracle. —Albert Einstein

Many years ago I set out on a quest to remember who I really was and live the life that I came here to live. This statement may seem a little "out there" but I always felt I had a purpose and I came to make a difference in this world. It wasn't just about me; it was that every one of us has a true reason for being here. Our job is learning who we really are and living that gift that has been given in our lives.

I've had these feelings since childhood and have always been drawn to spirituality. Even at a very young age, I would sit in stillness in church and see angels. I could walk into a room full of people and feel everything they were feeling, know what they were thinking, and where they were going. At that time, I thought everyone had these gifts of perception. I had such a knowingness that there was a deep beauty to life and a profound purpose that most often was not discussed in everyday life.

One Sunday I was praying in church and I noticed a woman a few pews back staring at me. After the service she came up to me and told how drawn she was to me because when I prayed there was a sense of peace and energy about me that moved her. She said she experienced this energy on her recent trip to Medjugorje, Yugoslavia, a place of many miracles where the Virgin Mary had often been sighted.

She repeatedly said, "You look like her, feel like her, like that energy." I thought clearly, "I'm not the Virgin Mary." I felt very uncomfortable with the whole interaction. However, she saw something in me and was sending me a message. She wanted to take my hand, look in my eyes, and tell me of her life and longings to open her heart more. I've had many experiences like this over the years.

Another time someone came up to me at a gathering and asked if I was familiar with the story of Mary Magdelene and her life in France and the Cathars. Afterwards, I read some of the writings about her and was so moved by her beautiful work. Interestingly, my great grandmother was from France and was a Cathar.

It has been a rich and challenging journey of seeking myself; over the years my identity has been gently revealed to me. Clearly, there is a feminine face of God and she is within every woman and man. I know now that I am of the Feminine Principal, the Yin, or unseen part of ourselves; the "being" part of us that is receptive. Yet I have had a lot to learn on the subjects of "being" and receptivity.

For me, this is not some far-fetched, mythological statement. I know that at my very core I remember a place of profound peace and a way of life that is based on love, respect, kindness, balance, and power shared, where people seek to empower themselves and others for the greater good. I have found and know a wavelength with God and my purpose here is to hold this myself and help others remember who they really are and find their way back to love.

My journey to remember who I am led me to a powerful spiritual training academy where I spent many years of spiritual studying, meditation, self-assessment, healing, and life's journey work. As I began to remember, I became a teacher, healer, minister, and counselor of this work which gives people tools to find themselves and the knowledge of who they really are. The work had brought me back to life, saved my life, and now I could pass the favor forward. I have studied with some brilliant teachers who had been so profoundly generous to me. My life was rewarding and purposeful.

Fourteen years after I began my in-depth spiritual journey, I was totally in love with Bourke, my college sweetheart and husband of twenty-one years. I adored my beautiful young son, Michael, and my amazing mother, Hazel, lived close by. I had pretty much anything the external world could offer at my fingertips.

Over the same fourteen years, I had also safeguarded my physical health as doctors tried to explain why I had occasional, mysterious physical symptoms. I would get tired sometimes and had tingling down my legs that would come and go. There were a lot of talented doctors with many different ideas and possible diagnoses; was it post-polio, multiple sclerosis, or lyme disease? Who really knew? During this time, I would not allow myself to be labeled and focused on healing and listening to what my body needed. The last doctor I saw called me "remarkable" a couple of times in the same sentence. He said perhaps these had all been misdiagnoses. I was grateful for feeling good and able to live my life.

In the summer of 2007, a car accident sent my life sideways. While driving to lunch one day my car was hit. The other vehicle was a huge black truck. The impact was intense. It felt like a bad dream. My body was so hurt, my brain was foggy, and I could barely put two words together. My balance was very shaky, my neck and back ached, my right leg stiffened, my right foot did not point and flex. Walking was difficult. At times I was paralyzed and my husband would carry me wherever I needed to go in the house. This independent, never-give-up girl was hurt.

It was a terrifying time physically, mentally, emotionally, and spiritually. Life was rough; my life as I knew it had changed forever. With all the trauma and pain, I held onto remnants of remembering myself and the depth of love that I felt from God. I used to say I was good friends with God; well, where was God now?

Where was the beauty and the peace in me? Everything felt like war. Over the course of the next two years we had to let go of our home. Our life savings and retirement savings were gone. My time was spent in appointments with doctors, physical therapists and lawyers. I could not work and was in tremendous pain. My husband worked day and night taking care of me, Michael, handling the household chores and working to pay the bills. All the things we had built financially for twenty years together had disappeared. I felt quite lost and abandoned by many, and especially God.

Where were the miracles that I used to regularly participate in? In the past, I could always meditate and find the solution to a problem, heal, and move forward. In my entire life, I always believed that if I worked hard enough I could do anything. Well this was something different. All the types of healing work and self-assessment I had learned were not working.

The internal dialogue began to sound like this; "Well, Ginette, if you are such a healer, why can't you heal yourself and get yourself out of this trauma?" The self judgment was heavy. The judgment from others reflected the judgment from within. I no longer felt velvety and beautiful; I felt defeated and lost. In truth, I was experiencing something that people endure after traumatic experiences like an accident, serious illness, surgery, or loss.

I had never experienced the depth that a person can freeze after trauma. There is a powerful book, *Waking the Tiger*, by Peter A. Levine, that speaks to this phenomenon in nature, with animals and humans and our innate capacity to heal and transform overwhelming experiences. I was humbled by feeling the experience of it all, or should I say the lack of feeling of it. I had lived the decade before this accident helping people wake up from a slumber; now I was frozen and the challenging thing is that for a long time, I was too frozen to know it.

I heard Christopher Reeves say once, "It's time to focus on our abilities instead of our disabilities." I know now that we all have disabilities and limitations of one kind or another that we can heal. Perhaps our heart aches and it's not physical; it's for the longing to be loved. Perhaps we are so frightened, we retreat into our minds and never allow ourselves to feel. Maybe we are challenged by being in relationships with others or we can't nurture ourselves. There are many types of disabilities, none better or worse. I happen to be healing a physical disability, which is quite visual to the human eye.

This empathic child became a very empathic grown woman; with all my tools and energetic systems I could still feel all the feelings and thoughts of those who would stare at me. It felt judgmental, sticky, and negative; their stares evaluated me as I would physically struggle. I just wanted to be free from all the projection.

Life Choices: Navigating Difficult Paths

One day I said to Bourke, "Some people's staring makes me feel vulnerable; it feels so awkward, invasive, and mean-spirited."

He said, "Yes, there are a lot of people who simply can't extend courtesy to anyone, Ginette, including themselves." What he said next really got me. "However, have you noticed all the people who are sending love your way as they see how courageous you are?"

I realized he was right; there were a lot of people who were kind. Those who were not were simply showing who they were at that moment and it really had nothing to do with me.

In my most challenged moments, Bourke would say, "Ginette, you are more than your right leg, more than your ability to walk. You are beautiful and that will never change." His tenacious words finally reached my heart and I started asking myself, "Is my mere value to be able to walk? Is that the only important thing in my life? Is it worth giving the rest of my glorious life away to despair?" I began thinking "Wow, being paralyzed can really get a girl down, but it can't keep me down!"

The idea came back to me again: We all have two choices; we can live our lives or we can die our lives, literally walking around in the process of slowly dying. In this period, my healing was coming back to life and realizing that to fully live I needed to let my old life die. Holding onto my old life was a form of dying.

At first I focused on healing myself to get me back to where I was, the way my life used to look, the way my body worked before the car accident. In essence, to grow backwards. But it was, and always is about growing forward. Every time I compared the now with the then, I was energetically linking myself to a place that had no power or truth anymore. It was simply the residual memory of who I was back then. As I began the process of letting the old me go, I began to be able to look at the history of my life this time and love me and accept me now. It was very freeing; I like to call it my 'present-past life memory.'

It was clear that this was a pivotal time in my life and I was approaching an important crossroad. If I went down one path, I would have a certain outcome; if I went down another road, there would be a totally different life. I knew the path I wanted was the one of heart and I knew that I would have to face my fears.

So, who heals the healer? I have most often been a person who supported and gave help to others. These days were different. I learned a lot about asking for help and receiving it. I must admit, some days I got there kicking and screaming. One of the valuable things I learned was letting go of control about what the help looked like or who God was sending to give the help. Each person brought something to my healing. As I started receiving help, it opened me to more and more healing, more options that are ever-changing and bring more assistance. I was starting to thaw.

A talented healer friend of mine said to me, "Ginette, you will make it through this. Just don't get caught in self-importance; it's dicey waters." What she was saying is that it was not so much about my back, hip, and physical walking. It was if I would be identified by the challenges or not.

One day I found myself listening to the physical therapist as she recommended I get a walker so that I could walk with safety. I recoiled as she spoke. I didn't need a walker, I'm a ballet dancer, an athlete! I've danced on the world's largest stage, been totally physically adept all my life.

Somehow, I felt that if I started walking with a walker that I had failed, not worked hard enough to heal, gave up on myself. It's quite interesting; I didn't want to walk with a walker because I was so afraid that I would never get well. When in truth, by using one, I was taking care of myself, giving myself a chance to heal. It was clearly time to get out of my own way.

This once again brought forward my ability to receive help. I seemed to know how to say the words to ask for help, but there's a difference between asking and then receiving it. I realized how this felt on the other side as people would ask for my help over and over again, take it, but not be able to receive it.

Good news. I was speechless at the caliber of people in my life. God was pulling out all the stops to help me. The cast of angels during this time were simply amazing; these beings were of the highest caliber of healer. My mother, the healer, brought her unconditional and enduring love of me, her life code of such honor and strength and the depth of her kindness and nurturing. She exemplifies the feminine face of God to me daily. My son, the healer, brought me such a powerful innocence, joy of life, and acceptance. His pure love lifted my heart. My husband, the healer, brought his unwavering strength of soul, his wisdom, his gifts of service, his ability to hold love for me at such a magnitude, and his ability to help me with perspective of truth. These beings stayed at my side daily and worked with me with such loyalty and love. Where was God? Right there shining through these remarkable people who just happened to be my family and friends.

This casting call of angels included my family, friends, and many amazing people who were brought into my life. Without question, my physical therapist, is an angel. She definitely knows who she really is. This woman is truly remarkable; she's the real deal and I needed someone like her—brilliant, loving, firm and totally talented as a healer. She has intense training in working with people after traumatic events like car accidents.

During a session one day more than a year after the accident, she asked me, "So when did you know you survived the accident?"

I lay there quietly for a while, and then answered, "I am not sure I did survive it. I feel like I have been walking around, not dead, but not alive either." As a teacher and a student who strives to fully feel, this kind of a statement was jarring. It was then that I realized just how traumatic and damaging the accident had been on my body, mind, and soul.

I left that day barely able hold myself together; when I got in my car, I began sobbing. There was such a physical release, a release of energy that had been very stuck. I felt all the stress and grief, the frustration, and most of all, I began to feel the thaw. I was starting to come out of the frozen state and had lots of feelings and tears coming up. What a relief.

When I could accept that I had been hurt, and it was not my fault, I knew that I had not let myself or God down. I felt this flooding of love and gratitude for myself and my courage to never give up, even through the most challenging times. It was then that I could say I don't care how I get there, I will get there. I don't care what it looks like on the outside. I will do this; I will get to that place of not being defined by the external. Then the turning point came; I didn't care what it looked like to anyone but God.

When I least expected it, I had the turning point—a great shift. It happened one day while auditing a class at the spiritual academy where I have studied for almost sixteen years. It was a profound time of sharing. There were a couple of hundred people participating and I had phoned in on a conference line. The geographical distance didn't matter, because I had such a sense of intimacy with God. When it was my turn, I shared a few feelings and then suddenly to my surprise, I started speaking to God out loud, really direct, really reaching. I said something like this: "God, I'm all in, everything that I am, everything that you made me, all the gifts you gave me, all the training and teaching to help others, all my brilliance, all my challenges. All of me that is healing, I bring my all to you."

It was a prayer of the greatest surrender that I have ever felt and I became fully committed to God. I still get chills when I think of that moment. I was so grateful to be witnessed by all those loving beings who were present there with me. In that moment I felt the turn in my life. It was like a powerhouse of light came into me and I have never been the same, forever changed. This has been the most profound time in my life. Through all of these challenges I had been gifted with a bigger perspective than I could have ever dreamt of and a vista of the greatness of life.

Since that moment, I started holding myself in a state of loving honor like never before. I belonged to God in the deepest meaning. As my healing journey continues, I have fallen in love with myself and my life in the most lushly authentic way. The garden of my life is blooming again; the flowers are new and fresh. I am humbled. I am a better mother, wife, daughter, friend, healer, student, and teacher because of this part of my journey. I don't fear the darkness anymore; I celebrate the light. I have a deep level of confidence, knowing that I am showing up for my life with my heart wide open and loving full out. Albert Einstein was right; we all have free will. I choose to see everything as a miracle—I'm living one.

About the Author

Ginette has held leadership, training, and coaching positions with an international non-profit organization, worked for several Fortune 500 companies and successfully created and managed her own award-winning entrepreneurial business for the past two decades.

Ginette has been a senior faculty member and senior counselor with the Training in Power Academy for over a decade. She is a senior minister with the Power of Spirit Church. Her work focuses on wellness, healing, meditation, and assisting others to the path of self-awareness.

Her interests are in vibration and transpersonal psychology, spiritual transformation, life potentiality, and the feminine face of God.

She holds a bachelor's degree from the University of Nevada, Las Vegas and is pursuing her master's degree in psychology.

Ginette presently lives in Las Vegas, Nevada in the richness of a three-generational household with her husband Bourke, son Michael Kealoha, and mother, Hazel.

Ginette Osier Bedsaul can be contacted at:
Ginette@Bedsauls.com

Invisible

REVEREND CHARLOTTE FOUST

All I wanted was to enter the sanctuary. I wanted to go inside to feel the peace and comfort I somehow knew was within. We weren't a religious family. I had never been inside a church, but I knew that the song I heard in my heart had something to do with what was inside that small white building with the cross on top … and yet, I was too small to go in.

I believe I am finally coming to terms with the realization that I would not be the person I am today had I not lived all of the lives that brought me to this point. To the casual observer, some of the paths I have taken in my life and the choices I have made would not appear to be the direction one would take to get here. As I look back I can see the reason for the turns and detours, the potholes, and mountains to be climbed along the way, all of which were a result of choices I made.

The desire to pursue the calling of my heart has been with me since before I had words for it. I've always 'known' there was something more … an overwhelming, all encompassing good. It has always seemed just beyond my reach. There were glimpses of light, moments of profound peace … yet they were fleeting.

Perhaps that is because of the choice I made early on to turn away, to close my heart to the song it longed to hear. No one would have thought such a minor incident would have had such a profound effect on a child. Some fifty-five years later, I can still see the sun reflecting off the new white paint. I can almost feel the breeze. In my darkest moments I can clearly hear the stern, commanding voice of the wrinkled old lady as she leaned into my face and said with a sneer, "You can't go in. You're much too small."

It was years later when I learned the reason I could not go in. It was an election day; the church was my parents' local polling place. Since I wasn't old enough to vote, I could not enter the place where the voting was taking place. It wasn't that I was too small, not worthy, lacking in any way—the runt of the litter, unacceptable to God. I simply wasn't old enough. By then it didn't matter that I learned the truth, I had made a choice—a choice to refuse to hear. I hadn't cried at those painful words so long ago; I had simply chosen to obey and walk away.

My childish mind had chosen to shut out what I wanted because I believed I couldn't have it. It was easier, I thought, to live in silence than to feel the emptiness which acknowledging the longing would bring, and the inevitable rejection that would come if I tried to follow my heart's desire. Instead, I consciously chose what I believed to be the easy way out.

I did everything I could to be invisible. I became a master stone mason, building impenetrable walls around the core of my being. I let no one in and the 'me that I longed to be' remained safely hidden behind my walls. It wasn't safe to venture out, to show people who I was inside. The once outgoing, bubbling, exuberant child learned to pretend.

I decorated my stone walls with happy faces, with the masks that allowed me to seem to be everything anyone wanted me to be. I wore my 'Charlie Face' like a badge of honor, telling the world I was successful and happy. Inside, I was alone, lonely and unfulfilled. I continued to make choices that would lead to even greater separation from self and a deepening, occasionally overwhelming, sadness. I not only built a wall to keep others out, I built a second wall to keep myself in, not realizing I was actually keeping myself OUT as well. I lived in the space between the walls.

I was lucky to have an older brother. Not because he was the kind of older brother you find on 50s television shows. Far from it. I was lucky because he was one of those boys who grew so fast his coordination skills couldn't keep up. Our pediatrician recommended ballet lessons. My mother agreed, but only on the condition that I, too, could take lessons. For my brother, it was like medicine, but I loved it from the very first lesson.

Then came my first recital when I was once again faced with a choice that would shape many years of my life. The recital was held in the high school gymnasium. It was BIG, at least to someone my size. I could hear the echo of those innocent words—you're too small. If I stayed out there on that floor all those people would see; they would know I was too small. I loved to dance, but I didn't want all of those people to see me. I wanted to be invisible. I cried—and ran off the floor before the dance started. I ran to my mother. She made my next choice very clear. I could either march myself back out there and do the dance—or I could quit dancing forever. I chose to dance.

It wasn't pretty; I cried and sniffed all the way through my performance. But perform I did. In my mind, I made myself invisible to everyone. I just shut myself inside. I danced. I danced for me ... for me only. I found solace in the rhythm and movement. The external music spoke to the emptiness inside.

Later I learned that as long as I kept quiet and did reasonably well in school, I could be invisible and escape to the dance studio. I chose to live in a world apart from most of my contemporaries. It was easier to add more bricks and mortar to the walls than to tear them down. I never fit in, never felt like I belonged anywhere except on the dance floor where I was free to be me.

Growing up, my brother and I took lessons every day after school, sometimes before school and all day on Saturdays. Sunday was family day. In our house that meant doing laundry, cleaning house, doing yard work, changing the oil in the car ... whatever it took to have everything ready for work, school, and dance classes for the coming week. I was busy, too busy to have time to think about making choices. I had become adept at ignoring the voice inside. As long as I didn't listen, I could pretend I wasn't too small. I didn't have to feel the pain of rejection. I didn't have to choose. The loneliness of silence became my friend. I allowed life to carry me along, shifting and turning in whatever direction someone pointed me, always marching to someone else's drum, never really choosing my path, allowing things to happen by default and using dance as my escape.

Life Choices: Navigating Difficult Paths

No matter how hard I tried, how fast I ran, how loud the music, the song in my heart never went away. I tried counseling, but I was never really honest with my counselor. I know he knew that. He was a patient soul, allowing me to find my own way. I tried church, and while there was some comfort there, I just didn't want to get into a conversation with God about whether or not it was ok for me to be there. I wanted to be there. I wanted the voice inside to break through. Every time I was close, I would run to hide again inside my walls.

Right out of high school, I left home and began an eight year career as a dancer in the flashy, glittery world of Las Vegas entertainment. It was there that I met the man I married.

April 11, 1982, was a turning point in my life. With friends in town, we decided to attend an Easter sunrise service. My son in the back seat with my friend and me, our husbands in the front, we headed up the mountain to greet the morning. The service, like most of my experiences in church, was pretty flat. I found nothing inspirational, nothing that resonated to the music inside. Nothing that could reach the 'me' I had buried so deep.

It was on the way back down the mountain, my friend said that she, too, was disappointed in the service. We had picked up a local publication on the way out of the lodge. Thumbing through the paper, she came across an ad for another church. It somehow spoke to both of us. As the guys had had enough church for the day, we decide that the two of us would go to the other service. We would have just enough time to drop them off and get there.

The major part of the service was a silent meditation. It was in that silence and the safety of the sanctuary that the voice in my heart clearly spoke to me, and for once, I listened. It said, "Welcome home; I've been waiting for you."

I'd like to be able to say that my walls instantly tumbled down and my life became one of contemplation, peace, and freedom, but not all life-changing moments create instant and lasting change. The habits of a lifetime are hard to break. Once outside the safety of the sanctuary, my own voices reminded me again that I was too small. The doubt set in and I argued with myself. With the encouragement of my friend and my counselor, I made my first conscious choice to explore a spiritual path.

Classes were difficult. In the beginning the best I could do was stop building new walls. As time went on, I began to see glimpses of light between the bricks. I took out bricks and put in windows … it was a start. There were, and still are, times when I put up shutters over my new windows.

I didn't make a choice every day. Sometimes it is easier to just go back to letting life happen. Breaking through the walls is tough. I discovered that every brick has its own life. None of them are going to just crumble and fall. I will have to tear them down, brick by brick … stone by stone. It wasn't until I had holes in the wall that kept people out that I found the wall I had built was keeping me out as well. I learned that before I could break free, I had to get IN.

I make choices now. Every day. Sometimes, from moment to moment. I strive to be consciously aware of the choices I make. I am a minister now. I've been a minister for a number of years. I know that everything I have experienced has led me to this place. I've learned to listen (most of the time) to my inner voice. I like to think that God and I have a pretty good relationship. In the past, I had doubts. I have gotten angry with God. I have ignored, yelled, cried, and hidden from that relationship.

For today, I choose to continue to chisel away at my walls. I choose to share. I choose to listen. I choose to hold on to that which someone said to me recently, "I see you." She didn't mean she saw me standing there. She meant she could see ME. It wasn't her words, but the light shining from her eyes that spoke volumes. She saw ME. I was shocked to realize, that if she could see me, God has always seen me … no matter how many walls I built or how successfully I thought I was hidden from view. Now, I'm learning to see myself. I choose to be visible.

Life is not about avoiding obstacles and challenges to sail happily into the sunset. It is also not about hiding from ourselves or being big enough. Life is about choice. Every day, every moment we have the opportunity to choose a new path. When we listen to the music of our hearts, the choices becomes easy. The choices we make determine the lives we live. Who we are now is the culmination of all we have been and the whole is greater than the sum of its past.

I have learned no matter what we choose, how many walls we build, or mountains we climb, when we are ready, God is waiting to welcome us home.

About the Author

Though her heart lives in the redwoods of northern California, Charlotte Foust's career as a dancer led her to make Las Vegas her home forty-two years ago. Before becoming executive assistant to a motivational speaker and author, the twists and turns of life took her through successful careers not only as a dancer, but also in sales and marketing, cosmetology, and the title and escrow industry. As the owner/director of a ballroom dance studio, she developed a program of creative and therapeutic dance for the intellectually challenged community of Las Vegas. She has enjoyed countless hours volunteering with Special Olympics, Children's Miracle Network, and numerous local Las Vegas organizations. Driven by the desire to find balance and harmony, she pursued spiritual studies throughout her journey, finally putting her on a path toward the ministry. Charlotte currently serves as associate minister of Unity Church of Las Vegas.

Charlotte Foust can be contacted at:
rev.charlotte@live.com

A Final Thought...

Things happen for a reason and we get through them as best we can. Hopefully, we learn from everything that happens. We are who we are because of all that has gone before and all of the choices we have made. We made the best of things as they were, with the knowledge and skills we had at the time. As we grow, have more experiences and learn more lessons, we are able to make different and better choices. We need to have faith that we will learn to make the choices that will get us where we want to be and obtain the success we desire.

These authors wrote their stories (even though in some cases it was extremely painful to do so) in order to give you the gift of hope and let you know that you do have choices ... just as they did.

We can begin to live a new life any day we choose. It doesn't mean our old lives go away. It means we've started down a new path. Developing new beliefs isn't always easy. We have to commit to it. We have to work at it every day. Like any other journey we may take, we will come across roadblocks, dead ends, and detours. We may even run out of gas. But we have the power to make the choice of which direction we will take and whether or not to complete the journey.

Life is a succession of choices. You have the ability to choose. Don't choose to spend your life wallowing in negativity, failure, ignorance, poverty, shame, or self-pity. Choose instead to let go of old hurts and old belief systems. Choose instead to raise your sights, develop new belief systems and reach for the success that you desire. Choose happiness, confidence, peace of mind, contentment, fame and/or fortune. Choose to navigate your difficult path wisely and you will meet with a success you never believed possible.

Life Choices Books

If you would like to order additional copies of *Life Choices: Navigating Difficult Paths*, please visit our website at www.lifechoicesbook.com or call 702-896-2228. Discounts are available on quantity orders.

Speakers

Most of the authors in this book are available for speaking engagements. If you would like to have one of them make a presentation for your organization, you may contact him/her at the contact address given at the end of the chapters or Turning Point International at (702) 896-2228.

Your Story

If you are an author or have a burning desire to tell your story, we are interested in working with you.

We are looking for stories that enlighten, inspire, motivate, or entertain. Each of our *Life Choices* books focuses on a specific topic or passion. *Life Choices* books contain well-written, original, non-fiction stories that include one or more of the following themes:

- Life lessons you have learned and the impact they've had on your life
- How you overcame an obstacle or met a life challenge
- How you or someone you know maintained a positive attitude in spite of life situations
- An experience of a synchronistic moment, a moment of "fate," or something awe-inspiring
- Random acts of kindness and the impact they had on your life

Contributing to an anthology such as this one is the fastest, easiest, and most affordable way to become published. Published authors are recognized as experts. This is a simple, easy way to quickly establish yourself as an expert and gain credibility.

Call (702) 896-2228 to find out about upcoming titles and how to submit your story.

Life Choices Authors
Other Products

BOOKS

Aimmee Kodachian
Tears of Hope
Riley Publications, Las Vegas, Nevada
ISBN: 0-9776135-0X

Jesse Ferrell
How You Leave Them Feeling
JessTalk Services, Las Vegas, Nevada
ISBN-10: 0-9778810-0-0-8

Mary Monaghan
Remember Me?
Tortoise Press
Cape Town, South Africa
ISBN: 978-0-620-36648-9

Elle Swan
"Your Mind Over Habits"
Swansense Publishing, Las Vegas, Nevada
ISBN: 978-0-615-28026-4

Anne Abernathy, six time Olympian, known as 'Grandma Luge'
50 over 50: Extraordinary Women, Extraordinary Lives
£15.99 hardback
Dewi Lewis Media Ltd (2007)
London

Anne Dreyer
Darling What Fork Do I Use?
Colourworks International
Pine Town, South Africa
ISBN: 978-0-62033-055-8

Darling I have Nothing To Wear?
Colourworks International
Pine Town, South Africa
ISBN: 0-620-33066-4

Edie Raether
Winning! How Winners Think...What Champions Do
Performance Plus Publishing
Terrell, NC, USA
ISBN: 1-931219-02-8

Forget Selling: 12 Principles of Influence and Persuasion in Sales, Leadership, and Life
Peformance Plus Publishing
Terrell, NC, USA
ISBN: 1-931219-03-6

Why Cats Don't Bark: Unleash Your PowerZone: Intuitive Intelligence-The Other I.Q.
Liberty Publishing Group
Raleigh - Frederick - Egg Harbor, USA
ISBN: 1-893095-14-2 (soft cover)
ISBN: 1-893095-17-7 (hard cover)

Sex for the Soul: Seven Secrets of Sensual Intimacy for Spiritual Ecstasy
Performance Plus Publishing
Terrell, NC, USA
ISBN: 1-931219-00-1

What Most Builders Won't Tell Women (or Men): 101 Ways to Save Big Bucks on Your Next Home
Performance Plus Publishing
Terrell, NC, USA
ISBN: 978-1-931219-07-5

I Believe I Can Fly! A Fun Adventure on Potential and Possibilities
Performance Plus Publishing
Terrell, NC, USA
ISBN: 978-1-931219-15-0

Sandra Neilsen
Sex and the Zen of Shopping
Tajine Publishing, Las Vegas
ISBN: 978-0-9842799-0-6

Sherial Bratcher
Blue Print for Success
Insight Publishing Sevierville, Tennessee
ISBN: 978-1-60013-210-0
ISBN 10: 1-60013-210-3

Karen Phillips
Discover Your Inner Strength
Insight Publishing, Sevierville, Tennessee
ISBN: 978-1-60013-387-9

Judi Moreo
You Are More Than Enough: Every Woman's Guide to Purpose, Passion, and Power
Stephens Press, Las Vegas, Nevada
ISBN-10: 1932173722

Achievement Journal
You Are More Than Enough
Stephens Press, Las Vegas, Nevada
ISBN 13: 978-1932173659

Ordinary Women, Extraordinary Lives
Career Press, Franklin Lakes, NJ
ISBN: 1-56414-701

Conquer the Brain Drain: 52 Creative Ways to Pump Up Productivity
National Press Publications,
Shawnee Mission, Kansas
ISBN: 1-55852-299-9

Ignite the Spark: 52 Creative Ways to Boost Productivity
Penguin Books, Johannesburg,
South Africa
ISBN: 0 143 02433 7

Mama's Rocking Chair
Patchwork Path, Grandma's Choice
Choice Publishing Group,
Las Vegas, Nevada
ISBN: 978-0-9816643-1-6

Shotsie, Career Cat
The Ultimate Cat Lover
HCI Books, Deerfield Beach, Florida
ISBN 13: 978-0-7573-0751-5

I'll Send You A Rainbow
The Ultimate Mom
HCI Books, Deerfield Beach, Florida
ISBN 13: 9780757307966

The Robin
The Ultimate Bird Lover
HCI Books, Deerfield Beach, Florida
ISBN 13: 9780757314384

AUDIO BOOKS

Casey McNeal
Building Relationships: How to Work With People
Sound Solutions   (6 CD's)
ISBN: 1-55852-377-4

Jesse Ferrell
How You Leave Them Feeling
PM Digital Group   (7 CD's)
ISBN: 9 780977881000 53695

Judi Moreo
You Are More Than Enough
Soundtrax (12 CD's)
Las Vegas, Nevada

MUSIC ALBUMS

Sandy Kastel
This Time Around
Silk and Satin Records, LLC, 2007

Only In Las Vegas
Silk and Satin Records, LLC, 2007

Indiana Rain
feature song 'Detour'
Silk and Satin Records, LLC, 2010